C000264544

PRAYING WITH CHRISTIAN MYSTICS

For Kieran

Annetta Maguire

Praying with
Christian Mystics

the columba press

First edition, 2013, published by
the columba press
55A Spruce Avenue, Stillorgan Industrial Park,
Blackrock, Co. Dublin

Cover by Bill Bolger
Origination by The Columba Press
Printed by MPG Print Group

ISBN 978 1 85607 721 7

Copyright © 2013, Annetta Maguire

Contents

Introduction

༅ ༅ ༅

Many of us today find ourselves searching for answers to our spiritual questions. This is evident by the fact that almost all bookshops have a section offering a large range of books of a spiritual nature, which hold out the promise of answering these questions. It is surprising to read of the array of manifestations available in Ireland today under the heading of 'spirituality' and the many non-traditional ways people are now approaching this. All offer help in finding answers to the age-old questions such as: who am I?; where did this all begin?

As we try to satisfy our spiritual needs in this way, we can easily find ourselves becoming spiritual tourists. This is not a new phenomenon; each generation naturally asks questions, and goes in search of answers. On my own spiritual journey I spent many years studying eastern philosophy, attending groups, practising transcendental mediation, learning Sanskrit and reading literature from the Vedanta tradition such as the Upanishads. Despite this study being mentally and spiritually enriching, I found after time that it was not addressing the heart of my questions and was, in fact, just going around in circles.

A friend suggested that I study my own Christian tradition in more depth. Thirty years ago when I began my quest for answers, courses for lay people were not readily available, whereas now this is not the case. After some enquiries I was accepted on a MA degree course in Applied Christian Spirituality at Milltown Institute in Dublin. This for me was a moment of grace for which I will ever be thankful. As I began the study I felt I was at last 'home' and soon realised how little I knew of my own rich tradition.

During the course I was introduced to the lives and works of some of our Christian mystics. Their names were vaguely familiar but I knew little or nothing of their lives or teachings. Through this study I discovered that a complete guide to a spiritual path leading to union with God was available through the writings of such people as St Teresa of Avila and St John of the Cross. These mystics had a strong desire for union with God and no obstacle, however difficult, could prevent them fulfilling their goal. They met with great suffering, both physical and mental, but were able to see the hand of God in all the events of their lives. Through their writings they have left a map, as it were, of their spiritual journey which led to unite with God. Reading their words it was possible to appreciate that their step-by-step directions, written between the thirteenth and the sixteenth century, were as relevant today as they were then.

Karl Rahner, the German theologian, wrote: 'The Christian of the future will be a mystic or he or she will not exist at all.'[1] Rahner rejected what he called an elitist interpretation of Christianity. Through my study of the Christian mystics I came to understand that whereas the various saints and mystics had written down their spiritual experiences and explained in great detail the path they had travelled, it was possible and indeed probable for so-called ordinary people to have spiritual experiences which were indeed 'mystical'. As these experiences were often not spoken about or recorded, it has become the norm to think only of mystics as those officially declared so by the church; these are mostly either ordained men or religious sisters.

Rahner wrote that there was a mysticism of everyday life, and this was available to all God's people. He explained that God does

---

1. Quoted by Declan Marmion in *A Spirituality of Everyday Faith* (Louvain: Peeters Press, 2007), p. 61

communicate himself to us all, all the time. This communication can, of course, be accepted or rejected but the fact remains that God is present in the office, in the school, in the kitchen or wherever we find ourselves at any given moment. Thus, Rahner 'moves away from an understanding of mysticism as limited to those who are technically called mystics in the Christian tradition'.[2] As a lay woman reading these words I had the desire to come to a fuller understanding of what it meant to be a mystic. St John of the Cross wrote: 'God carries each person along a different road, so that you will scarcely find two people following the same route in even half of their journey to God.' Accepting that each of us is different, I had the sense that through their writings the mystics could act as guides for us as we make our own very unique journey to God. By reading and studying their lives and teachings we could be inspired to emulate their courage and faith. Life today can indeed be stressful, and reading the lives of the mystics we can see that they too had to face difficulties, but because of their faith they were able to transcend the problems they met and leave to posterity teachings full of joy and hope.

In the following pages I have given a brief outline of the life of four Christian mystics whose writings I have found inspirational. I also include some passages for reflection from their writings. The value in giving a set of reflections for each mystic is to allow us to see in practice if the guidance given by the mystic can have relevance in our ordinary day-to-day life. From these reflections it will be possible to decide if you want to continue reading their writings in greater depth.

Reading the passages for reflection can provide both spiritual inspiration and spiritual guidance. It is important to read the words slowly to allow them to touch you personally, to speak directly to you. Words can lead us back to the source and provide nourishment for our whole being. While reading the passages be aware of your inner responses. Ask yourself: Do I agree with what is being said? If so, take a moment to acknowledge this. If you do

---

2. Ibid., p. 62

not understand, or you disagree with something, also mark this. You may find that each time you read a passage your understanding deepens.

Words need to come alive and for this to happen it is necessary for us to breathe life into them. We do this by attending fully and listening deeply. This can only happen if we allow ourselves time. The journey inwards to self discovery begins with body-awareness. For this we need first to practise to be still physically. The exercise given before each set of reflections will help with this.

By allotting time each day for moments of stillness, followed by spiritual reading and reflection, we are feeding our inner being, thus providing a balance for our physical, mental and spiritual bodies and allowing ourselves to discover spiritual rest, which is often missing in today's busy world.

Julian of Norwich

Julian of Norwich
1342–1416

Julian of Norwich introduces us to a loving, kind and courteous Jesus. Her appeal as a mystic lies in her complete optimism, her faith that every person is loved by God, and this is expressed in her writings. To her, everything is good because God is good. Despite receiving what she called *Divine Revelations*, Julian did not regard herself as special, but believed what was revealed to her was for everyone. She was chosen by God, not because she was special but to pass on the message of his great love for us. She continually assures us that if we have faith we shall not be overcome by the trials of this life, no matter how difficult life appears. She had complete trust in the words of Jesus when he said to her, 'all will be well … you will see for yourself that every kind of thing will be well.'

Julian lived in fourteenth-century England, a time of turbulence in church and state. Although the events were different, the states of chaos and despair were not unlike our situation today. It was the time of the Black Death and the Peasants' Revolt, a time when the church was in disarray with no less than three men claiming to be the true pope. Reform was also much needed in society where there was a thirst for social equality and for an end to slavery and serfdom. It is in this context that Julian spent her life of solitude, contemplation and prayer. In spite of the problems of the time, her conviction in the truth of God's love for all was the one thing that made sense to her. Because of this love she was able to see things differently as is evident from her writings. Her words may be a help to us today.

Very little is known about Julian of Norwich outside of the fact that she lived as an anchoress. An anchoress was a sort of recluse confined to a small house or single room, often attached to the side of a local church. As an anchoress, she chose to live a life set apart from the world, dedicated to prayer and devotion to God. In order to become an anchoress she needed the permission of the local bishop. Having obtained permission, she was required to go through an elaborate ceremony which included her receiving the Last Rites. At the end of the ceremony the door of her room was bolted from the outside. She would remain in this room for the rest of her life. There were three windows in the room: one opening into the church so she could hear Mass, one for her servant to pass in food and take away any waste products, and one opening on to the street where people could come to seek spiritual advice. As an anchoress, Julian would offer prayers of intercession for the people of Norwich.

The women who dedicated themselves to God during the Middle Ages seem to have been less numerous than the men, but they were not less influential. Like the monks, they were of two kinds: nuns living in communities and hermitages, and anchoresses living alone. The communities mostly had less than ten members, very different from the large communities of nuns and monks which were in existence in the nineteenth or twentieth century.

In the fourteenth and fifteenth centuries, men and women who sought to be alone with God had an enormous impact on the people of the area precisely because they were able to achieve divine solitude. They fulfilled a social function of praying, counselling, reconciling, settling political conflicts and also fulfilled the role of teaching.

It is not known when Julian became an anchoress, if it was before or after she received the Divine Revelations. However, this is unimportant as it is her words and the words she said were spoken to her by Jesus that are important. Julian's book *Revela-*

tions (*Showings*) *of Divine Love* was the first book of spiritual instruction in English written by a woman, indeed no woman before had written any book in any language. Julian's reason for writing was that she was sure the message was not just for her. She wrote: 'this vision was shown for all men and not for me alone.'[1] For Julian this understanding of what she had received was so important that she left everything and spent the next twenty years reflecting on the meaning of what she had experienced, committing them to writing with a view to passing on her insight into God's love to others.

When Julian was thirty and a half years old, between 4 a.m. and 9 a.m. of 8 May 1373 she received fifteen visions, with a sixteenth during the next evening. These sixteen visions make up the short version of *Revelations of Divine Love*. They were written with the details fresh in Julian's mind. For the next twenty years Julian continued to reflect on what she had seen and heard and then wrote the longer version which consisted of eighty-six chapters that reflect her deeper insight into her original experience.

Julian leaves us an account of what happened the day of The Revelations. She writes:

> When I was thirty and a half years old, God sent me a bodily sickness in which I lay for three days and three nights, and on the third night I received all the rites of holy church, and did not expect to live until day. After this I lay for two days and two nights, and on the third night I often thought that I was on the point of death, and those who were with me often thought so too. And yet in this I felt a great reluctance to die, not that there was anything on earth which it pleased me to live for, or any pain of which I was afraid, for I trusted in the mercy of God. But it was because I wanted to live to love God better and longer, so that I might through the grace of that living have more knowledge and

---

1. Unless otherwise stated all quotations from Julian are from *The Classics of Western Spirituality* edition: *Julian of Norwich (Showings)*, trans. Edmund Colledge OSA and James Walsh SJ (NY: Paulist Press, 1978). Future references will indicate in brackets after each citation page number and short or long text. (p. 136, ST)

love of God in the bliss of heaven. But it seemed to me that all the time that I had lived here was very little and short in comparison with the bliss which is everlasting. I thought: Good Lord, can my living no longer be to your glory? And I understood by reason and the sensation of my pains that I should die; and with all the will of my heart I assented to be wholly as was God's will.

My curate was sent for to be present at my end; he set a cross before my face, and said: 'I have brought the image of your Saviour; look at it and take comfort from it.'

So I lasted until day, and by then my body was dead from the middle downwards, as it felt to me … After this my sight began to fail. It grew as dark around me in the room as if it had been night, except that there was ordinary light trained upon the image of the cross, I did not know how.

After this the upper part of my body began to die, until I could scarcely feel anything. My greatest pain was my shortness of breath and the ebbing of my life. Then truly I believe that I was on the point of death. Suddenly at that moment all my pain was taken from me, and I was as sound, particularly in the upper part of my body, as ever I was before.

(p. 179–180, LT)

At this point she had a series of fifteen visions, or 'showings', in which she was led to contemplate the Passion of Christ. These brought her great peace and joy. Her mother and her priest were in the room at the time but they did not see anything.

Her visions were mostly of the passion of Christ. Such visions were not uncommon among recluses and might have been dismissed as of no special significance except for herself, had they been all that happened. However, with them were associated 'showings' which she received in her 'understanding' and which continued for many years after the visions of the passion had ceased. As she herself puts it: 'All this was shown in my understanding, and by spiritual intuition.'

In the longer version Julian spent most of her time reflecting and praying on the meaning of the showings as she could not understand what Jesus meant when he said:

> I may make all things well, and I can make all things well, and I
> shall make all things well, and I will make all things well; and
> you will see for yourself that every kind of thing will be well.
>
> *(p. 151, ST)*

Julian had difficulty understanding these words as she had been
brought up to believe that sin was our own fault and that we
would be punished for it. This she understood was the teaching
of holy church. But she says:

> This, then was my astonishment, that I saw our Lord God show-
> ing no more blame to us then if we were as pure and as holy as
> the angels are in heaven.
>
> *(p. 266, LT)*

Julian's revelations strongly suggest that the 'all' that will be
well in God's promise includes 'every particular human being',
although this is never stated absolutely. She states:

> He dwells here in us, and rules us, and cares for us in this life,
> and brings us to his bliss. And so he will do as long as any soul is
> on earth who will come to heaven; and so much so that if there
> were no such soul on earth except one, he would be with it, all
> alone, until he had brought it up into his bliss.[2]

Julian is helped by the fact that she understands that there is
a 'deed' ordained by our Lord God which is known only to himself, through this deed he will make all things well. She writes
that Jesus told her:

> There is a deed which the Blessed Trinity will perform on the last
> day, as I see it, and what the deed will be and how it will be per-
> formed is unknown to every creature who is inferior to Christ,
> and it will be until the deed is done.
>
> *(p. 232, LT)*

For twenty years less three months after the time of the 'showings' Julian reflected on what she had seen and heard and then
she says the Lord answered very mysteriously, by revealing a

---

2. Joan Nuth, *Wisdom's Daughter* (NY: Crossroads Publishing Co., 1991), p. 164.

wonderful example: the parable of The Lord and the Servant. Julian wrote an account of this:

> I saw two persons in bodily likeness, that is to say a lord and a servant: and with that God gave me spiritual understanding. The lord sits in state, in rest and in peace. The servant stands before his lord, respectfully, ready to do his lord's will. The lord looks on his servant very lovingly and sweetly and mildly. He sends him to a certain place to do his will. Not only does the servant go, but he dashes off and runs at great speed, loving to do his lord's will. And soon he falls into a dell and is greatly injured; and then he groans and moans and tosses about, and he cannot rise to help himself in any way. And of all this, the greatest hurt which I saw him in was lack of consolation, for he could not turn his face to look on his loving lord. Then this courteous lord said this: 'See my beloved servant, what harm and injuries he has had and accepted in my service for my love, yes, and for his good will. Is it not reasonable that I should reward him for his fright and his fear, his hurt and his injuries and all his woe? And furthermore, is not proper for me to give him a gift, better for him and more honourable than his own health could have been? Otherwise, it seems to me that I should be ungracious.'

> *(p. 267–268, LT)*

Julian tells us:

> The servant who stood before the lord was shown for Adam, that is to say, one man was shown at that time and his fall, so as to make it understood how God regards all men and their falling. For in the sight of God all men are one man, and one man is all men.

> *(p. 270, LT)*

Julian says that God imputes no blame to the servant. However, the servant is unaware of this as he cannot turn his face to look on his loving lord and this is his real pain, he is now only aware of his failure and cannot know how his lord has responded to his failed mission, and as a result he has lost all sense of his own goodness. He is now in misery. Julian lists his seven great pains: bruising, clumsiness, weakness, forgetfulness, he could not rise, he was alone and the place was narrow and comfortless. (pp. 267–268, LT)

The sin in the parable of the lord and servant is that the servant is now only aware of the physical suffering he has and that becomes his 'world'. And all the time the lord was so close to him. Julian tells us, 'God is closer to us than our own soul, for he is the foundation on which our soul stands.' (p. 288, LT)

This parable is for Julian a powerful reminder of the great love Jesus has for us. It helped to explain his words when he said 'Sin is necessary but all will be well, and all will be well, and every kind of thing will be well.'(p. 225, LT) If when the servant falls he could see the whole picture he would realise there is no need for him to feel guilty that indeed all is well, the lord is very near to him.

In the parable we hear that the servant stands for each and every one of us; this being the case, it allows us to look at ourselves with the eyes of God and to experience the joy of knowing ourselves as the object of God's love. Another important point that Julian makes is that Jesus says to her, 'What is impossible to you is not impossible to me.' (p. 233, LT) He asks her to accept everything he says with faith and trust 'and in the very end you will see truly, in fullness of joy'. (p. 232, LT)

The most important part of Julian's teachings is her ability to question and reflect, however long it took her to understand. She speaks from her heart, her relationship with Jesus is, as she says herself familiar, and she speaks to him as to a beloved friend not a figure of authority. She says, 'Thus I chose Jesus for my heaven. No other heaven was pleasing to me than Jesus, who will be my bliss.' (p. 143, ST) She is in no doubt about her own salvation and reading this part of her message encourages us not to be afraid of the future but rather to rejoice in this present moment which, seen through the eyes of Julian, is filled with God.

Julian ends her book with a prayer that her work may fall only into the hands of those who wish to love God. Given the religious climate of the time, where anyone who displayed independent thinking was in potential danger of being burnt at the stake for heresy, Julian's work was undertaken with considerable risk. This accounts, at least in part, for the obscurity which enveloped her writing for so long. It also helps explain her sense of caution about the readership of *The Revelations* and makes her accomplishment all the more remarkable.

From the time of her visions in 1373 Julian spent many years puzzled over the question: What was our Lord's meaning in revealing these things to me? At the end of this long journey, she receives the answer:

> Jesus said: Do you wish to know your Lord's meaning in this thing? Know it well, love was his meaning. Who reveals it to you? Love. What did he reveal to you? Love. Why does he reveal it to you? For love. Remain in this, and you will know more of the same. But you will never know different, without end. So I was taught that love is our Lord's meaning. And I saw very certainly in this and in everything, that before God made us he loved us, which love was never abated and never will be.
>
> (p. 342, LT)

Julian was then able to understand that God wants his love for us to be better known and this was why the meaning was revealed to her. Julian informs us that her work began as 'God's gift and grace' but that, at the time of writing, 'it is not yet performed'.

More than six centuries later, it is now the task of those who have experienced the grace, beauty and power of her words to ensure that her book and the passionate love of God that it depicts is 'performed' fully and widely.

Julian is a mystic who can speak to people in the twenty-first century, a time of unease and spiritual doubt for many. She herself lived through such a time; she is speaking from personal experience when she tells us we cannot understand God with the mind we have to love. Her significance as a mystic and theologian is widely recognised. Thomas Merton was devoted to her. Writing of her he said: 'Julian is without doubt one of the most wonderful of all Christian voices. She gets greater and greater in my eyes as I grow older. I think that Julian of Norwich is with Newman the greatest English theologian.'[3] In the writings of Julian we are shown a very loving and kind Jesus, intent on our happiness and well-being, a friend for us in all areas of our life.

Through her writings, Julian promises, no matter how things appear now there will come a time when everything will make sense. She reveals a world where everything, even sin, is transformed, into love. To put on the mind and heart of Julian what is needed is to love. It is easy to imagine her giving comfort and warmth to all who called to her window seeking spiritual guidance.

---

3. Thomas Merton, *Seeds of Destruction* (NY: Farrar, Straus and Giroux, 1980), pp. 274–5.

Passages for reflection from
Revelations (Showings) of Divine Love

Preparation for reading passages for reflection:

- Choose a quiet place and a quiet moment
- Sit in a comfortable relaxed position
- Close your eyes
- Be aware of the silence and stillness around you.
- Just rest in this awareness for a minute or so.

Take one passage at a time to reflect on. While reading the passages be aware of your inner responses, as these are your own personal connection with the text.

1st Passage for reflection:

Jesus said, 'I may make all things well, and I can make all things well, and I shall make all things well, and I will make all things well; and you will see for yourself that every kind of thing will be well.'

Exercise:
Become aware of how these words affect you.
Can you relate what Jesus is saying to your personal experience? Note your response.

2nd Passage for Reflection:

It was a great marvel, constantly shown to the soul in all the revelations, that our Lord God cannot in his own judgement forgive, because he cannot be angry – that would be impossible. For this was revealed, that our life is all founded and rooted in love, and without love we cannot live. I saw most truly that where our Lord appears, peace is received and wrath has no place; for I saw no kind of wrath in God, neither briefly nor for long. For truly, as I see it, if God could be angry for any time, we should neither have life nor place nor being. (263–264, LT)

Exercise:
What line in this passage resonates with you?
What does it say about God's attitude to each of us?

3rd Passage for reflection:

This is a longer passage so take it slowly. Read a paragraph at a time and then sit with this for a moment to reflect on its meaning for you. Remember that Julian understands that her experience is also ours.

Our Lord opened my spiritual eyes, and showed me my soul in the midst of my heart. I saw my soul as wide as if it were a kingdom, and from the state which I saw in it, it seemed to me as if it were a fine city. In the midst of this city sits our Lord Jesus, true God and true man. I saw him splendidly clad in honours. He sits erect there in the soul, in peace and rest, that is. The humanity and the divinity sit at rest, and the divinity rules and guards, without instrument or effort.

The place which Jesus takes in our soul he will nevermore vacate, for in us is his home of homes, and it is the greatest delight for him to dwell there. This was a delectable and a restful sight, for it is so in truth forevermore; and to contemplate this while we are here is most pleasing for God, and a great profit to us. And it was a singular joy and bliss for me that I saw him sit, for the contemplation of this sitting revealed to me the certainty that he will dwell in us forever; and I knew truly that it was he who had revealed everything to me. And when I had contemplated this with great attention, our Lord very humbly revealed words to me, without voice and without opening of lips, as he had done before, and said: 'Know it well, it was no hallucination which you saw today, but accept and believe it and hold firmly to it and you will not be overcome.'

These last words were said to me to teach me perfect certainty that it is our Lord Jesus who revealed everything to me. He did not say: 'You will not be assailed, you will not be belaboured, you will not be disquieted', but he said: 'You will not be overcome.' God wants us to pay attention to his words, and always to be strong in our certainty, in well being and in woe, for he loves us and delights in us, and so wishes us to love him and delight in him and trust greatly in him, and all will be well. (p. 163–165, ST)

> *Exercise:*
> What do you understand by the words: 'The place which Jesus takes in our soul he will nevermore vacate'?
> Jesus said, 'You will not be overcome.' Would trusting in these words make a difference to your life?
> Knowing that 'God wants us always to be strong in our certainty, in well being and in woe, for he loves us and delights in us', does hearing these words give you courage when faced with problems?

4th Passage for reflection:

Our Lord showed me a spiritual sight of his love. I saw that he is to us everything which is good and comforting for our help. He is our clothing, for he is that love which wraps and enfolds us, embraces us and guides us, surrounds us with his love, which is so tender that he may never desert us. And so in this sight I saw truly that he is everything which is good. (p. 130, ST)

> *Exercise:*
> Can you trust that Jesus will never desert you?
> Does anything else strike you about this passage?

5th Passage for reflection:

I had great longing and desire of God's gift to be delivered from this world and from this life. For often I beheld the pain that there is here and the good and the blessed being that there is there; and if there had been no pain in this life except the absence of our Lord, it seemed to me sometimes that that was more than I could bear.

And to all this our courteous Lord answered: 'Suddenly you will be taken out of all your pain, all your sickness, all your unrest. And you will come up above, and you will have me for your reward, and you will be filled full of joy and bliss. Why then should it afflict you to endure awhile, since it is my will and to my glory?' And in these words: 'Suddenly you will be taken', I saw that God rewarded us for the patience which we have in waiting God's will and his time. This is very profitable, because if we knew when the time would be, we would set a limit on our patience. Then, too, it is God's will that so long as the soul is in the body it should seem to us that we are always on the point of being taken. For all this life we have here is only an instant of time, and when we are suddenly taken into bliss out of pain, then pain will be nothing. It is God's will that we focus our thought on this blissful contemplation, as often as we can and for as long as we can continue in it with his grace, for to the soul who is led by God, this contemplation is blissful and greatly to God's glory while it lasts.

(p. 305–307, LT)

Exercise:

What is your immediate response to hearing Julian speak of her desire to be delivered from this world?

How do you respond to Julian saying it is blissful to contemplate that we are always on the point of being taken to God?

6th Passage for reflection:

God wants us to understand and to believe that we are more truly in heaven than on earth. Our faith comes from the natural love of our soul, and from the clear light of our reason, and from steadfast memory which we have from God in our first creation. And when our soul is breathed into our body, at which time we are made sensual, at once mercy and grace begin to work, having care of us and protecting us with pity and love, in which operation the

Holy Spirit forms in our faith the hope that we shall return up above to our substance, into the power of Christ, increased and fulfilled through the Holy Spirit. So I understood that our sensuality is founded in nature, in mercy and in grace, and this foundation enables us to receive gifts which lead us to endless life. For I saw very surely that our substance is in God, and I also saw that God is in our sensuality, for in the same instant and place which our soul is made sensual, in that same instant and place exists the city of God, ordained for him from without beginning. He comes into this city and will never depart from it, for God is never out of the soul, in which he will dwell blessedly without end. (p. 287, LT)

Exercise:
What effect does it have for you to hear that 'God wants us to understands and to believe that we are more truly in heaven than on earth'?
What is your understanding of Julian's words: 'our substance is in God'?

Finally:
Take some time to reflect on how reading and studying passages from Julian's reflections on *Revelations of Divine Love* can help you on your own personal spiritual journey.

⊘ ⊘ ⊘

For further study:

Julian of Norwich (Showings) (Classics of Western Spirituality), trans. Edmund Colledge OSA and James Walsh SJ (New Jersey: Paulist Press, 1997)

Nuth, Joan M., *Wisdom's Daughter* (New York: The Crossroad Publishing Co., 1991)

St Teresa of Avila

St Teresa of Avila
1515–1582

Teresa of Avila was declared a doctor of the Church by Pope Paul VI on 27 September 1970. She was born on 28 March 1515 in Avila into a family which was among the minor nobility of Spain. Her father, Don Alonso Sanchez de Cepeda, was one of the wealthiest men in Avila. Writing of him, Teresa said he was a man of great devotion and very conscientious. She wrote of his high principles by telling how he refused to own slaves and described how, when her uncle sent one of his slaves to stay with her family for a short time, her father treated the girl not as a slave but as a family member. She thoroughly approved of this, but as having slaves was the normal practice at the time, this must have marked him out among his neighbours as an eccentric.

Teresa's family were of Jewish origin and as this was the age of the Spanish Inquisition and descendants of converts from Judaism were often investigated on suspicion of continuing to practice the Jewish faith, her family came under some suspicion on account of their Jewish ancestry.

In 1505 Alonso married, but two years later his wife died leaving him with two children. He married again and Teresa was one of ten children born to this marriage, thus Teresa grew up surrounded by a large family of sisters and brothers. Her mother died when she was fourteen. In the story of her life she describes a happy childhood. Biographers have given us a detailed description of her; in many ways an extrovert, she was cheerful and friendly, a good conversationalist, and people found her pleasing to hear as well as to look at. Teresa wrote that she had a strong desire to be appreciated by others. She was sensitive to criticism and eager for admiration. At the age of sixteen she had a mild flirtation with one of her male cousins which caused small scandal in the town and following this her father decided to sent her to an Augustinian convent to be educated.

Since there was no public education system in Spain at the time, Teresa probably learned to read and write at home. Women were not admitted to the universities, or to other centres of study, nor were they allowed to read vernacular writings on spirituality. Teresa in her time protested against these restrictions. Later she would become a champion of women's culture, and when she founded a new movement to reform the Carmelites, all the sisters had to be able to recite the divine office and assist in choir. However, Teresa, true to her nature, wanted to include all, and relaxed this rule when an illiterate girl came to the convent. Teresa herself taught the girl to read and write.

During her time in the Augustinian convent the nuns did little more than prepare the young girls for their future life in marriage, teaching them needlework, cooking etc. The nun who had charge of the girls was a very devotional woman who loved to talk about prayer. Her high spiritual ideals made a deep impression on the young Teresa. She wrote how she loved to hear the good and holy conversation of this nun telling how the Lord rewards those who give up all for him. At that time Teresa began to think about a vocation. However, ill health forced her to leave the school. Throughout Teresa's life she suffered from fairly continuous ill health. In the story of her life she wrote that she could hardly remember a day without pain. When she died at the age of sixty-seven it was not possible for the doctors to say for sure what she had died from; her body had become a whole arsenal of ailments.

For Teresa, the idea of a vocation remained strong and at the age of twenty she stole away from her father's house and without his permission went to the Carmelite monastery of The Incarnation in Avila. Teresa later wrote: 'When I left my father's house

I felt the separation so keenly that the feeling will not be greater, I think, when I die.'[1] Her father, however, accepted her decision and gave her a dowry that was more than substantial and acquired for his daughter a private room of her own in the monastery, with a servant to look after her. When Teresa entered the convent up to two hundred women were living there including servants and relations of some of the nuns. It was not an enclosed convent and, as Teresa found, there was ample opportunity for the nuns to leave the convent for social as well as other reasons. A class structure existed in the convent and there were varying lifestyles according to whether the girl was wealthy or not. It was possible to actually buy rooms, with the best rooms going to the richer girls. The poorer girls slept in dormitories. Even from the colour of their religious garb it was possible to tell which social class they came from. At the time it was not unusual for girls to enter the convents as a solution to a social problem rather than in response to a religions vocation. Teresa was aware of all this and later when she set about her reform of the Carmelites she insisted on equality at all levels for the nuns.

Once in the monastery Teresa threw herself into the life with zest and found that it, in fact, delighted her. But shortly after her profession, which took place two years later, her health gave way once more. After three years during which she experienced much suffering at the hands of various doctors, some of whom were quacks, she returned to the convent.

After nineteen years spent in the convent in 1554 she had a profound spiritual conversion which changed her life forever. In *The Book of Her Life* she describes this event:

> It happened that one day entering the oratory I saw a statue they had borrowed for a certain feast to be celebrated in the house. It represented a much wounded Christ and was very devotional so

---

1. Unless otherwise stated all quotations from Teresa are from *The Collected Works of St Teresa of Avila*, trans. Kieran Kavanaugh OCD and Otilio Rodriguez OCD (Washington: ICS Publications, 1987). Further references will indicate in brackets after each citation page number and volume. (p. 18, vol. I)

that beholding it I was utterly distressed in seeing him that way, for it well represented what he had suffered for us. I felt so keenly aware of how poorly I thanked him for those wounds that, it seems to me, my heart broke.

(p. 101, vol. I)

This conversion dislodged the egoism that had hindered her spiritual development. Thus, at the age of thirty-nine, she began to enjoy a vivid experience of God's presence within her. She also experienced a deepening of this conversion when reading *The Confessions of St Augustine*. She wrote about this occasion:

As I began to read the *Confessions*, it seemed to me I saw myself in them. I began to commend myself very much to this glorious saint. When I came to the passage when he speaks about his conversion and read how he heard the voice in the garden, it only seemed to me, according to what I felt in my heart, that it was I the Lord called.

(p. 103, vol. I)

Following these two spiritual experiences Teresa placed all her trust in God and from then on trusted him and not herself at all times.

From 1556 on, unfamiliar, unusual experiences started to occur and Teresa, not yet enlightened about the stages of prayer, wrote that at this time she began to be afraid. She thought that these experiences may have been caused by the devil. At that time in Spain there were reports of women who had been deceived in this way.

Teresa lived at a time when there was a culture of delighting in the extraordinary. People believed that God was speaking to them and that they were having visions. Self-deception and self-projection were rife. John of the Cross wrote: 'Furthermore, persons having these apprehensions often develop secretly a special opinion of themselves.' He is very clear in his warning about looking for or setting store by phenomena when he states: 'Whatever does not engender humility, charity, mortification, holy simplicity, silence, and so on, of what value is it?' John teaches that 'Faith is fullness, and phenomena are less than fullness'.[2]

Teresa was fully aware of the situation of possible deception and so decided to reveal all to her confessor and hold nothing back. She also came to the conclusion that she should obey her confessor whatever he said. However, she found that on obeying all his directions, the spiritual experiences in fact increased. Following on from this, her confessor instructed her to write down all her experiences. This instruction led to her writing the story of her life.

Writing the story of her life, Teresa devotes chapter twenty-two to explaining a difficulty she herself experienced in her prayer life. She tells how she read some spiritual books which make the case that as one's prayer life develops it is better to rid oneself of all corporeal images. 'They say that in the case of those who are advancing, these corporeal images, even when referring to the humanity of Christ, are an obstacle or impediment to the most perfect contemplation and that one should try to think of God in a general way, that he is everywhere, and that we are immersed in him.'[3] Teresa says that as she had no master at the time; reading these books made her believe that her understanding of contemplation was developing. She decided to turn away from all corporeal images of Christ. She thought the humanity of Christ was an impediment to her spiritual development. When she looks back at this time in the story of her life she writes:

> At no time do I recall this opinion I had without feeling pain; it seems to me I became a traitor – although through ignorance. I saw clearly afterwards that God desires that if we are going to please him and receive his great favours, we must do so through the most sacred humanity of Christ, in whom he takes his delight.
>
> (*p. 192, vol. I*)

---

2. Iain Matthews, *The Impact of God* (London: Hodder and Stoughton, 1995), p. 100.

3. Iain Matthews, *The Impact of God* (London: Hodder and Stoughton, 1995), p. 191.

She goes on to write that the most sacred humanity of Christ must not be counted in a balance with other corporeal things. 'Christ is a very good friend because we behold him as man and see him with weaknesses and trials and he is company for us. Once we have the habit, it is easy to find him present at our side.' (p. 196, vol. I)

For Teresa, Christ was the centre of her mystical life; in the book of her life she writes:

> We should occupy ourselves in looking at Christ who is looking at us, and we should speak and petition ourselves, and delight in the Lord's presence. When we can do this, even though it may be at the beginning of prayer, we will derive great benefit; and this manner of prayer has many advantages – at least my soul derived them.
>
> *(p. 133, vol. I)*

One of the visions which Teresa describes in this story is of a beautiful angel appearing to her. In his hand he held a large golden dart and at the tip of the dart was a little fire. Teresa wrote:

> It seemed to me this angel plunged the dart several times into my heart and that it reached deep within me. When he drew it out, I thought he was carrying off with him the deepest part of me; and he left me all on fire with great love of God. The pain was so great that it made me moan, and the sweetness this greatest pain caused me so superabundant that there is no desire capable of taking it away; nor is the soul content with less than God.
>
> *(p. 252, vol. I)*

Teresa goes on to ask God in his goodness to give a taste of this love to anyone who may think she is lying.

As time went on Teresa desired to live a more contemplative life. The lifestyle at the Monastery of the Incarnation at this time was not conducive to keeping the Carmelite rule as perfectly as possible. Teresa wrote:

> Even though there were many servants of God in the house where I was, and he was very well served in it, the nuns because of great necessity often went out to places where they could stay. Also the

rule was not kept in its prime rigor. It seems to me the monastery
had a lot of comfort since it was a large and pleasant one.

(p. 280. vol. I)

Teresa herself left the convent on a regular basis as she had a
large circle of friends including members of the nobility who re-
quested her presence during times of illness or childbirth, which
meant she spent long periods of time away from the convent.

Teresa's desires for the contemplative life became known in
the monastery. She discussed with some other nuns the possibility
of founding a monastery in the ancient tradition of Carmel. This
convent would be home for no more than twelve nuns. All twelve
would share friendship with each other with no one excluded.
Teresa wrote: 'Let us understand, my daughters, that true perfection consists in love of God and neighbour; the more perfectly we
keep these two commandments the more perfect we will be. This
mutual love is so important that I would never want it to be forgotten.' (p. 295, vol. I) In the convent they would live in true religious poverty. Their lifestyle would be modelled on the simplicity
and austerity of the original Carmelites who developed from a
single community of men living as hermits on Mount Carmel in
Palestine in the early days of the thirteenth century. They are said
to have taken their inspiration from the prophet Elijah.

At first Teresa's confessor, the provincial of the Carmelites, and
other advisers encouraged her in the plan but when the proposal
became known among the townsfolk, there was a great outcry
against it. Teresa wrote: 'Hardly had the knowledge of it begun
to spread throughout the city when the great persecution that
cannot be briefly described came upon us: gossip, derision, saying
that it was foolishness.' (p. 281, vol. I) It is not easy today to understand how Teresa's decision caused such trouble in Avila.
However, at the time, the life of the communities centred around
the churches and monasteries. The richer classes and nobility
were patrons and considered it their right to disapprove of any
such changes. There was also the opinion that Teresa should be
grateful for the life she was enjoying in the convent, that wanting
to change things came from arrogance on her part. On account of

all the disapproval, the provincial of the Carmelites would no longer support the project. Five months later there was a change of rector at the Jesuit college; this had the effect of allowing her confessor to give his approval again. Immediately Teresa got one of her own sisters who lived outside the city to buy a house and fix it up as though it was for herself. This house was in fact to serve as Teresa's first reformed convent. The reason for this action was that Teresa wanted to avoid further outcry from the people of the town who objected to her plans. Many more difficulties would arise before the convent opened and Teresa was elected as the first prioress.

By 1577 the Carmelite reform developed from the first convent in Avila, The Monastery of St Joseph, to the establishment of fourteen houses from Burgos in the north of Spain to Seville in the south. All this necessitated a great amount of travel and ceaseless work for Teresa.

She spent the last years of her life travelling all over Spain, becoming famous and organising her fledgling convents and monasteries. Teresa established a completely new branch of the Carmelite Order, the Discalced Carmelite (meaning 'unshod' as they wore rope sandals of the poor in place of shoes). The order was for both nuns and friars. The reform of the friars started when Teresa met with St John of the Cross who would later become famous for his mystical poetry and writings. In 1926 he too was declared to be a Doctor of the Catholic Church.

In the last years of her life, Teresa desired to live a life of poverty, silence and solitude. However, in 1571, the Carmelite Provincial decided that Teresa should go back to the Convent of The Incarnation in Avila and become its prioress. The nuns there objected to this decision as they had always elected their prioress. Teresa had no wish to return either but, as always, she decided that to obey was the best course. On her return she managed to straighten out the convent's finances and organise matters so that the nuns had sufficient resources to maintain the convent. She also encouraged them with their spiritual practices. Towards the end of the story of her life Teresa wrote:

I now observe as though from up high and am really little bothered by what they say or know about me. God has given me a kind of sleep in life, or it almost always seems to me that I am dreaming what I see. I am aware in myself of neither happiness or pain, however great. This is the complete truth, for even though afterward I may want to rejoice over happiness or be sad about pain, it is not in my power to do so. The Lord has now awakened my soul from that which, because I was not dead to the world, caused me such feelings; and his majesty does not want my soul to become blind again. This is the way I now live.

(p. 362, vol. I)

Teresa was aware of her talent to write of her spiritual journey in such detail. She wrote: 'For it is one grace to receive the Lord's favour; another to understand which favour and grace it is, and a third, to know how to describe and explain it. All do not possess the charisma to speak of the unutterable mystical experience.' (p. 36, vol. I) Those who knew her testified that reading her words was like hearing her talk; the effect was the same, her manner of writing being the equivalent to her way of conversing. (p. 40, vol. I) As she had so many ideas and so many aspects of her spiritual life to write about, Teresa once said she wished she could write with both hands at the same time.

In giving personal testimony to her own experience, Teresa proceeds from her particular case to what can be said on a universal plane. In addition to a personal testimony, then, we have a teaching suitable for all. In giving her testimony she examines and analyses her spiritual life, making an extraordinary effort to explain herself, and this truthfully and with simplicity. She tells of the good things and the bad. The real object is to tell of the supernatural, to witness to the existence and the value of the realities of her inner life and to affirm their excellence and importance for all. She never attempts to camouflage her ignorance nor does she need to. She frankly admits the problem she has with explaining herself clearly in writing that she does not know philosophy and theology. Nor does she even have for her use as much as a Bible. This was the time of the Spanish Inquisition and the

Inquisitor General had forbidden many spiritual books as it was thought that they were harmful to the simple people. Teresa felt this very much as she thought reading these books was very helpful to her spiritual progress. She wrote that when the books were forbidden she heard the Lord say to her, 'Don't be sad, for I shall give you a living book.' She did not understand what this meant at first but later wrote: 'I understood very clearly, because I received so much to think about and such recollection in the presence of what I saw, and the Lord showed so much love for me by teaching me in many ways, that I had little or no need for books.' (p. 226, vol. I) So that, irrespective of her lack of means, she has certitude, the certitude of incontestable experience. She writes: 'I know through experience that what I say is true.' (p. 39, vol. I)

As prioress, Teresa was responsible for the spiritual care of many sisters. Her main concern was to help these nuns to develop their prayer life. In one of her most famous analogies Teresa uses the image of a garden to demonstrate the journey of the soul to God. She describes the soul as being like a garden given to us by the Lord to cultivate. At the beginning the garden is on very barren soil and full of weeds. The Lord pulls up the weeds for us and plants good seeds and then we have to play our part, and start to tend the garden, and get the plants to grow and not wither. She writes that there are four ways in which a garden can be watered:

> You may draw water from a well (which is for us a lot of work). Or you may get it by means of a water wheel and aqueducts in such a way that it is obtained by turning the crank of the water wheel. This method involves less work than the other, and you get more water. Or it may flow from a river or stream. The garden is watered much better by this means because the ground is more fully soaked, and there is no need to water so frequently and so much less work for the gardener. Or the water may be provided by a great deal of rain. For the Lord waters the garden without any work on our part and this way is incomparably better than all the others mentioned.
>
> *(p. 113, vol. I)*

This analogy shows how at the beginning praying can seem laborious and even tedious, but if we persevere, little by little things become easier and we come to realise that we in fact have to do nothing, that it is the Lord who in truth does the work for us.

In 1577, speaking to her confessor regarding the things of the spirit that she had written about in the book of her life, which was now in the hands of the Inquisition, she was asked to recall what she had written and to write another book. Teresa did not have any desire to do this but she held firmly to her belief: 'Obedience usually lessens the difficulty of things that seem impossible.' (p. 266, vol. I)

Teresa conceived the notion of using the castle as a symbol of the interior life. Her confessor later wrote that she told him that God showed her in a flash the whole book. She wrote:

> There was a most beautiful crystal globe like a castle in which were seven dwelling places, in the seventh, which was in the centre, the King of Glory dwelt in the greatest splendour. From here he beautified and illumined all those dwelling places to the outer wall. The inhabitants receive more light the nearer they are to the centre.
>
> *(p. 268, vol. II)*

The Interior Castle or *Book of Mansions* contains the essence of St Teresa's doctrine on prayer. It is considered to be her greatest work and there is good evidence for thinking that she considered it so herself. It was written when she was sixty-two years old, five years before her death.

A very brief description of the various mansions in the castle is as follows:

First Dwelling Place: Little of the glowing light from the King's chamber filters into these first dwelling places. People here have some good desires and pray sometimes. Too many things entice and distract souls here and thus prevent them from taking the time to search for the true light.

Second Dwelling Place: People here have taken steps in the practice of prayer, and are more receptive to the promptings and invitation of Christ's grace which comes especially through external means such as books, sermons, good company and through trials.

Third Dwelling Place: Those who have come to this stage begin to long not to offend his majesty; they guard against sin, are fond of ascetical practices, seek to use their time well, practise charity towards their neighbour, and maintain balance in the use of speech and dress and in the management of their household. Like the young man in the gospel, however, they could turn away upon hearing the requirements for becoming perfect. They need someone who is free of the world's illusions with whom they might speak.

Fourth Dwelling Place: The beginning of the supernatural or mystical stage. The important thing here is not to think much but to love much, and so do that which best stirs you to love. Love does not consist in great delights but in desiring with strong determination to please God in everything, in striving, insofar as possible, not to offend him. The contemplative prayer begins with a passive experience of recollection, a gentle drawing of the faculties inward. One should let the intellect go and surrender oneself into the arms of love, finding rest in the prayer of quiet, in the peace of God's presence. It is not unusual for souls to enter here.

Fifth Dwelling Place: The prayer of union characterises these rooms, an experience in which the faculties become completely silent. Leaves the certitude that the soul 'was in God and God was in it'. The soul becomes dead to itself and its attachments, and breaks free from its cocoon transformed as does a small butterfly. Love here is not idle, one so intimate with his majesty must walk with special care and attentiveness in the exercise of virtue and with particular emphasis on love of neighbour and humility.

Sixth Dwelling Place: Though the spiritual betrothal takes place in these rooms, the desires of the soul at a cost to itself must first increase. Through both vehement desires for God and the sufferings these desires cause, the Lord enables the soul to have the courage to be joined with him and take him as its spouse. The Lord shows the soul heavenly secrets. Some are so sublime that the soul is incapable of explaining anything about them; others can be explained to some extent.

The Seventh Dwelling Place: At this point 'the butterfly' dies with the greatest joy because its new life is Christ. In St Paul's words: 'The soul that is joined or united to the Lord becomes one spirit with him', 'for me to live is Christ'. The ultimate goal, then, of Teresa's journey, the spiritual marriage, is union with Christ. The fruit of spiritual marriage must be good works. The interior calm fortifies these persons so that they may endure much less calm in the exterior events of their lives so they might have the strength to serve. The works of service can be outstanding ones but they need not be. One must concentrate on serving those who are in one's company. The Lord does not look so much at the greatness of our works as at the love with which they are done. (270–278, vol. II)

Teresa admits when she started writing *The Interior Castle* she did so with aversion but when she finished the work it brought her much happiness. Teresa would continued to work and write tirelessly up to the time of her death in 1582 at the age of sixty-seven.

From reading or reflecting on the writings of St Teresa it is clear she was a born leader and organiser. Throughout her life she met with many, many difficulties, and had continuous bad health. Through all this she remained practical and down to earth, and wrote how she told the nuns 'not to be sad when obedience draws you into involvement in exterior matters. Knowing that if it is in the kitchen, the Lord walks among the pots and pans helping you both interiorly and exteriorly.' (p. 120, vol. III) She was to discover that setting up the reformed convents and monasteries was very unpopular with almost everyone. She had to face the Inquisition several times, but on each occasion she was found not to have been guilty of any error against the teachings of the church. A record of the judgement of one of her censors reads: 'Although this women is mistaken in some matters, at least she does not intend to lead others into error, for she speaks frankly of good and bad, and with such desire to be correct in what she says, that one cannot doubt her good intention.' (p. 47, vol. I) Teresa was able to meet all this with great courage and fortitude. It is evident that this courage did not come from any human source but from her personal faith that Christ was leading her and directing every aspect of her life and work.

Teresa's life and writings have inspired many people over the years. They continue to be a rich source of spiritual knowledge for those in Teresa's own tradition and also people from other traditions who desire to develop their prayer life. She is a good friend to those who want a deeper relationship with Jesus as she writes in great detail about how her own relationship with him unfolded. Should you wish to continue your study of this great mystic the recommended reading is *The Collected Works of St Teresa of Avila*, which are in three volumes, translated by Kieran Kavanaugh OCD and Otilio Rodriguez OCD.

In 2015 the Carmelite community around the world will celebrate the fifth centenary of the birth of St Teresa. It is their intention that throughout their communities people be encouraged to read the writings of St Teresa and they, in turn, encourage others to do the same. It is understood that Teresa's message and teaching is relevant today in all cultures.

◌ ◌ ◌

The Collected Works of St Teresa of Avila

Volume I: *The Book of Her Life*
               Spiritual Testimonies
               Soliloquies

Volume II: *The Way of Perfection*
               Meditations on the Song of Songs
               The Interior Castle

Volume III: *The Book of Her Foundations*
               Minor works

Passages for reflection from the writings of St Teresa of Avila

Preparation for reading passages for reflection:

- Choose a time when you are not likely to be disturbed.
- Sit comfortably and relaxed.
- Close your eyes.
- Be aware of the silence and stillness around you.
- Just rest in this awareness for a minute or so.

🖋 🖋 🖋

1st passage for reflection

Whoever has not begun the practice of prayer, I beg for the love of the Lord not to go without so great a good. There is nothing here to fear but something to desire. Even if there be no great progress, or much effort in reaching such perfection as to deserve the favours and mercies God bestows on the more generous, at least a person will come to understand the road leading to heaven. And if one perseveres, I trust then in the mercy of God, who never fails to repay anyone who has taken him for a friend. For mental prayer in my opinion is nothing else than an intimate sharing between friends; it means taking time frequently to be alone with him who we know loves us. (p. 44, vol. I)

Exercise:
What is your first impression having read this passage?
Teresa describes prayer as 'an intimate sharing between friends'. Does this description help in your understanding of prayer?

2nd passage for reflection

> In *The Interior Castle* Teresa wrote how she saw our soul as a beautiful
> crystal globe like a castle in which there were seven dwelling places,
> and in the seventh, which was in the centre, the King of Glory dwelt
> in the greatest splendor. From there he beautified and illumined all
> those dwelling places to the outer wall.

The Interior Castle: Words from the first dwelling place
We should consider our soul to be like a castle made entirely out
of diamond or of very clear crystal, in which there are many
rooms, just as in heaven there are many dwelling places. For reflecting upon the soul carefully we realise that the soul of the just
person is nothing but a paradise where the Lord says he finds his
delight. It is a shame and unfortunate that through our own fault
we do not understand ourselves or know who we are. It would
show ignorance if someone when asked who he was did not
know, and did not know his father or mother or from what coun-
try he came. We are incomparably more so when we do not strive
to know who we are, but limit ourselves to considering only
roughly these bodies. Because we have heard and because faith
tells us so, we know we have souls. But we seldom consider the
precious things that can be found in that soul, or who dwells
within it, or its high value. All our attention is taken up with the
plainness of the diamond's setting or the outer walls of the castle,
that is these bodies of ours.

  If this castle is the soul, clearly one does not have to enter it
since it is within oneself. How foolish it would seem were we to
tell someone to enter a room he is already in. But you must understand that there is a great difference in the ways one may be
inside the castle. There are many souls who are in the outer court-
yard. They do not care at all about entering the castle, nor do they
know what lies within that most precious place, nor who is
within, nor even how many rooms it has. The door of entry to this
castle is prayer and reflection. (p. 283, vol. II)

Exercise:

Can you relate to Teresa image of the soul as being like a beautiful crystal globe?

Is it true that our attention can be taken up by considerations of our physical bodies?

3rd passage for reflection

The soul is capable of much more than we can imagine, and the sun that is in this royal chamber shines in all parts. It is very important for any soul that practices prayer, whether little or much, not to hold back and stay in one corner. Let it walk through these dwelling places which are up above, down below, and to all sides, since God has given it such great dignity. If it is in the room of self-knowledge, how necessary this room is, even for those whom the Lord has brought into the very dwelling place where he abides. For never, however exalted the soul may be, is anything more fitting for it than humility.

Knowing ourselves is something so important that I would not want any relaxation ever in this regard however high you have climbed into the heavens. It is foolish to think that we will enter heaven without entering into ourselves, coming to know ourselves. In my opinion we shall never completely know ourselves if we do not strive to know God. (p. 291, vol. II)

Exercise:

The passage tells us that the room of self-knowledge is very necessary. What does this mean to you?

Do you think the soul is capable of much more than we can imagine?

Teresa often stresses the need for humility. How important is this virtue for you?

Teresa writes: 'In my opinion we shall never completely know ourselves if we do not strive to know God.' How do you understand this statement?

4th Passage for reflection

The following passage, taken from St. Luke's Gospel, is very familiar to most people. The story is of two sisters entertaining a guest. We have all had this experience when guests arrive; we want to give them of our best and this includes getting them something to eat and drink. Someone has to go to the kitchen to prepare the food, otherwise nobody will eat. In the story this person is Martha. Her sister remains with their guest. It seems the most natural thing in the world for Martha to feel she has pulled the short straw. She takes her case to Jesus; and so the story unfolds. The story can be understood at many levels. There is something of Martha and Mary in all of us and this is how Teresa understands the parable.

The Interior Castle: Words from The Seventh Dwelling Place

Let us desire and be occupied in prayer not for the sake of our enjoyment but so as to have strength to serve. Mary and Martha must join together in order to show hospitality to the Lord and have him always present and not host him badly by failing to give him something to eat. How would Mary, always seated at his feet, provide him with food if her sister did not help her? His food is that every way possible we draw souls that they may be saved and praise him always ... You need not be desiring to benefit the whole world but must concentrate on those who are in your company, and thus your deed will be greater since you are more obliged toward them ... We should not build castles in the air. The Lord does not look so much at the greatness of our works as at the love with which they are done.

Delight in the interior castle since without anyone's permission you can enter and take a walk through it at any time. Once you get used to enjoying this castle, you will find rest in all things, even those involving much labour, for you have the hope of returning to the castle which no one can ever take from you. (p. 448–451, vol. II)

Exercise:

When reflecting on the story of Mary and Martha is it possible for you to see something of both in action your life?

What is your understanding of the words of Jesus when he says: 'Mary has chosen the better part'

Teresa writes: 'You need not be desiring to benefit the whole world but must concentrate on those who are in your company.' What does it mean, 'those in your company'?

It is not the greatness of our works but the love with which they are done that is important. Do you agree?

5th Passage for reflection

The following passage is from *The Way of Perfection* and shows the very human side of St Teresa as she writes of having her good and bad days.

Sometimes I think I am very detached; and as a matter of fact when put to the test, I am. At another time I will find myself so attached, and perhaps to things the day before I would have made fun of, that I almost don't know myself. At other times I think I have great courage and that I wouldn't turn from anything of service to God; and when put to the test, I do have this courage for some things. Another day will come in which I won't find the courage in me to kill even an ant for God if in doing so I'd meet with any opposition. In like manner it seems to me that I don't care at all about things or gossip said of me; and when I'm put to the test this is at times true – indeed I am pleased about what they say. Then there come days in which one word alone distresses me, and I would want to leave the world because it seems everything is a bother to me. (p. 187, vol. II)

Exercise:

Does it help to understand that even a great saint like St Teresa can have these experiences?

In your own life do you notice how some aspects of your behaviour can change from day to day?

6th passage for reflection

Read and reread this short poem. The poem is full of understanding and meaning, and also spiritual direction. It is clear from her writings that Teresa herself fully realised the last line of the poem: that 'God alone is enough'. Having reflected on these words you may find they come to mind when you need them.

> Let nothing upset you,
> let nothing startle you.
> All things pass;
> God does not change.
> Patience wins
> all it seeks.
> Whoever has God
> lacks nothing:
> God alone is enough.

(p. 386, vol. III)

Exercise:
'All things pass': do you agree with this statement?
'Patience wins all it seeks': Is this your experience?
Finally, the line 'God alone is enough': Is it possible at this moment in your life to agree with this statement?

Finally:
After undertaking the various reflections from the writings of St Teresa of Avila take some time to consider how her words and teaching may assist you on your spiritual journey.

🖉 🖉 🖉

For Further Study:

The Collected Works of St Teresa of Avila, trans. Kieran Kavanaugh OCD and Otilio Rodriguez OCD (Washington: ICS Publications, 1987)

St John of the Cross

St John of the Cross
1542–1591

Saint John of the Cross was declared Doctor of the Universal Church in 1926. This Carmelite saint has left to the world writings and poems which contain some of the most profound mystical truths ever written. He is considered one of Spain's greatest lyric poets.

At the time of John's birth, Spain, a superpower, was suffering from widespread poverty and deep social discrimination. John's father Gonzalo de Yepes came from a wealthy family of silk merchants in Toledo. On a business trip to the town of Fontiveros he met and fell in love with Catalina, an orphaned girl from a poor background. They married and Gonzalo's merchant family disinherited him for his disloyalty to the family in marrying a girl from a low social class. At the time it was very much frowned on to marry outside your class structure. Gonzalo's family would never accept this marriage.

Three sons were born to the couple: Francisco, Luis and the youngest Juan who is known to us now as St John of the Cross. When John was two years old his father died. His widowed mother was reduced to poverty. As a last resort, seeking help, she went to visit the wealthy members of her husband's family but was again rejected by them. Shortly afterwards John's brother Luis died and Catalina and her two sons moved to Medina del Campo, a market centre in Castile where the family continued to live in poverty; Catalina made whatever money she could by continuing to work as a weaver.

John received an education when he entered a school in the city set up to educate disadvantaged children. From an early age John was a very talented student, eager to learn. From here, at the age of fifteen he worked as a nurse-cum-porter in one of the city's hospitals which cared for people suffering from contagious diseases. Thus, John spent his adolescent years discovering his gift of compassion for others as he cared for the sick. Through his work in the hospital he had further experience of suffering. Instead of making him cynical and hard this experience of suffering had the effect of opening his heart to God and to his fellow human beings.

In the hospital John came to the notice of the hospital's administrator who arranged for him to further his studies by enrolling in the local Jesuit school. After his studies it was thought that John would join the Jesuits, but, surprisingly at the age of twenty-one, John entered the Carmelites. With his novitiate year completed he moved to Salamanca where he studied theology and philosophy. Salamanca at that time had one of the best universities in Europe with large numbers of students from all over Spain. Here John continued to be regarded as a very bright student. In July 1567 John was ordained as a priest of the Carmelite order.

During his first year as a priest John became dissatisfied. Like Teresa of Avila before him, he had a desire for a purely contemplative way of life. His thoughts turned to the Carthusians. All changed, however, when in the autumn of that year he met Madre Teresa de Jesus (Teresa of Avila). Hearing about his aspirations toward more solitude and prayer and his thought of transferring to the Carthusians, she pointed out to him that he could find all he was seeking without leaving 'Our Lady's order'. She told him of her work reforming the Carmelite order to bring it back to its contemplative origins. With her characteristic zeal and friendliness she spoke to him of her plan to adapt this way of life for friars also.[1] Teresa was later to say that she started the reform of the friars with one and a half friars, John being the half friar – this on account of his small stature – however, Teresa also said, 'even though he is small, I understand him to be huge in the eyes of God.'[2]

John joined Teresa on a trip to Valladolid the following year where she was setting up a new foundation. He remained with Teresa for several months to learn the Teresian way of life. This was to inspire John to set up the first monastery for discalced Carmelite friars. The opposition to the reform of the Carmelites that Teresa had met continued and for John the outcome of this was that on the night of 2 December 1577 he was kidnapped by a group of Carmelites and lay people opposed to the reform, and who believed him to be guilty of crimes against canon law. He was taken blindfolded to a monastery in Toledo.

> His accusers locked him first in the monastery prison, but at the end of two months, for fear of escape, they moved him to another spot, a room narrow and dark, without air or light except for whatever filtered through a small slit high up in the wall. The room was six feet wide and ten feet long. There John remained alone, without anything but his breviary, through the terrible cold winter months and the suffocating heat of summer. Added to this were the floggings, fasting on bread and water, wearing the same bedraggled clothes month after month without being washed; and the lice.
>
> In the midst of this deprivation, John was seeking relief composing poetry, thus leaving to posterity some of the greatest lyric stanzas in Spanish literature. In that cramped prison, stripped of all earthly comfort, he was touched with some rays of divine light.
>
> *(p. 19)*

---

1. Unless otherwise stated all quotations from St John are from *The Collected Works of St John of the Cross*, trans. Kieran Kavanaugh OCD and Otilio Rodriguez OCD (Washington: ICS Publications, 1991). Further references will indicate in brackets after each citation the page number. (p. 13)
2. Iain Matthews, *The Impact of God* (London: Hodder and Stoughton, 1995), p. 8.

After nine months John made a miraculous escape. He managed to loosen the screws of the lock on the door of his cell and when all were asleep he made a rope from strips of his bed covers and escaped over the wall of the monastery taking with him various poems which he had written during his captivity.

After his escape from Toledo, John went to one of Teresa's communities in Beas de Sugura. The nuns there were shocked at his frail condition but were glad to have him with them and to nurse him back to health. John never spoke about what he had endured and bore no animosity towards those who had imprisoned him.

When Teresa took up duties as prioress at the Incarnation in Avila, John, who had by now taken the name of John of the Cross, joined her. He became spiritual director to the large number of nuns there, including Teresa herself. Later when Teresa's term as prioress of the Incarnation ended John stayed on as spiritual director. Over the next years John founded seven new monasteries for friars in the south of Spain.

However, their remained continued unrest in some quarters due to the unpopularity of the reform of the Carmelites, and John once again found himself embroiled in this. In the summer of 1591 a major meeting in Madrid showed up serious differences of opinion in the Teresian reform (Teresa herself had died in 1582). John objected to some of the policies and at the end of the meeting he found himself without a position or voice in running the reform. Instead, John was to lead a mission to Mexico with twelve other friars. John as always felt no bitterness at what had happened; in a letter written by him to the prioress in Segovia at this time he said:

> Do not let what is happening to me, daughter, cause you any grief, for it does not cause me any. Men do not do these things, but God, who knows what is suitable for us and arranges things for our own good. Think nothing else but that God ordains all, and where there is no love, put love, and you will draw out love.
> *(p. 22)*

John was never to go on the mission. In September, he developed an inflammation of his leg. At first this did not seem too serious. However, when it persisted he decided to seek medical attention in Ubeda. The prior of the monastery in Ubeda was not happy with the arrival of John. The man needed care and this would mean expense which the monastery could ill afford.

> John's sickness grew worse. His leg already ulcerated, and the disease, erysipelas, had spread to his back. On 13 December, Fray John of the Cross, knowing the time was running short, called the prior and begged pardon for all the trouble he had caused. This profoundly changed the prior, who himself then begged forgiveness and left the cell in tears, totally transformed. At midnight, without agony, without struggle, John died, repeating the words of the psalmist: 'Into your hands, O Lord, I commend my spirit.'
>
> (p. 23)

John was forty-nine years old at the time of his death.

✎ ✎ ✎

The Writings of St John of the Cross

The Ascent of Mount Carmel
Commentary on poem 'The Dark Night'

The Dark Night
Commentary on poem 'The Dark Night'

The Spiritual Canticle
Commentary on poem 'The Spirit Canticle'

The Living Flame of Love
Commentary on poem 'The Living Flame of Love

The Ascent of Mount Carmel
John was first of all a poet. He wrote books as commentaries on his poems when the friars, nuns and also the clergy and lay people who received spiritual direction from him asked for an

explanation of one or other of the poems he had given them. He wrote how he was reluctant to explain the poems as they were about matters so interior and spiritual for which words are usually inadequate. Both *The Ascent of Mount Carmel* and *The Dark Night* are commentaries on John's poem *The Dark Night*. At the beginning of each book John promises to comment on all eight verses of the poem but never got past verse two in either book.

It would be necessary to read the two commentaries in full to appreciate the meaning John gives the first two verses. I will just mention a few points which may be useful when reading the poem. John said his spiritual journey took place when his senses had been subdued; when he was fired with longing for union with God. In verse two he describes faith as the secret ladder. And the entire journey took place only through grace, as he states, 'ah, the sheer grace'.

The Dark Night of the Soul

1. One dark night,
fired with love's urgent longings
– ah, the sheer grace! –
I went out unseen,
my house being now all stilled.

2. In darkness, and secure,
by the secret ladder, disguised,
– ah, the sheer grace! –
in darkness and concealment,
my house being now all stilled.

3. On that glad night,
in secret, for no one saw me,
nor did I look at anything,
with no other light or guide
than the one that burned in my heart.

4. This guided me
more surely than the light of noon

to where he was awaiting me
– him I knew so well –
there in a place where no one appeared.

5. O guiding night!
O night more lovely than the dawn!
O night that has united
the Lover with his beloved,
transforming the beloved in her Lover.

6. Upon my flowering breast
which I kept wholly for him alone,
there he lay sleeping,
and I caressing him
there in a breeze from the fanning cedars.

7. When the breeze blew from the turret,
as I parted his hair,
it wounded my neck
with its gentle hand,
suspending all my senses.

8. I abandoned and forgot myself,
laying my face on my Beloved;
all things ceased; I went out from myself,
leaving my cares
forgotten among the lilies.

(p. 50)

John made a sketch which he called 'Mount Carmel' and said
it would serve as a summary of the doctrine contained in his book
The Ascent of Mount Carmel. (p. 113) The sketch shows the side of
a mountain with three paths going up to the top.

On the sketch 'Mount Carmel' the middle path is straight and
narrow and goes right up to the top of the mountain. On either
side are two other paths. Each much broader than the middle
path; both these paths stop far short of the top.

On the middle path, called the path of the perfect spirit, the
word *nada*, meaning 'nothing', is written all the way up and even
on the Mount. But this path opens out to a rich place. Here we

find the words: 'I brought you unto the land of Carmel to eat of its fruit and good things.' (Jr 2:7) Only the honour and glory of God dwells on this Mount. At the summit of the Mount there is nothing left but the law of love. Here there is no longer any way because for the just person there is no law as they are now a law unto themselves. It is obvious what John is saying here: the law exists only for those who are likely to break it. For the just person it is not the law that stops them from stealing etc., but their own virtue.

The right-hand path is marked: 'The way of the imperfect spirit in goods of the earth.' The left-hand path is marked: 'The way of the imperfect spirit in goods of heaven.' Written on the path of earthly goods are the words: 'The more I desired to seek them the less I had.' On the path of heavenly goods are written the words: 'The more I desired to possess them the less I had.'

It is easy to think that desiring heavenly goods is indeed praiseworthy, but not in John's eyes. To cling to little bits of spiritual insight or emotional sweetness holds up our progress in the present. John wrote: 'The fly who clings to honey hinders its flight, and the soul that allows its attachment to spiritual sweetness hinders its own liberty and contemplation.' (p. 87) He also says that if people are seeking spiritual consolation or favours from God they might have what he called a 'spiritual sweet tooth'. 'They still feed and clothe their natural selves with spiritual feelings and consolations instead of divesting and denying themselves of these for God's sake.' (p. 170)

The image of ascent as used in the Bible is always at a time when some transformation is about to take place. In Exodus, Moses ascends the mountain to speak to God and to receive the ten commandments. In the New Testament the Sermon on the Mount begins: 'And seeing the multitudes he went up into a mountain.' The transfiguration takes place when 'Jesus took Peter, James and John up into a high mountain'. John says the soul has to ascent 'to the summit of the mount, that high state of perfection we call union of a soul with God'. (p. 113)

The narrow path leading up to the top of the mountain is marked by the Spanish word *nada*, meaning 'nothing'. For John 'nothing' means giving up all desires. The only valid desire is for union with God. From his sketch, it is clear that to reach the summit all attachments have to be surrendered. It is important to realise that it is the attachment that has to be surrendered; whether it is to family, wealth, talents, etc. The attachment is the cause of the pain.

> We are not talking about giving up things, because that does not strip the soul, if its affective drive remains set on things. We are talking about stripping away the cravings for gratification in things. That is what leaves the person free and empty in their regard, even though they still own them. Because it is not the things of this world that take up space in the person and do them harm. No, it is the will and the hunger for them that dwells inside them.[3]

So John can write: 'To reach satisfaction in all desire satisfaction in nothing.' (p. 150) The path of the perfect spirit is simply: nothing, nothing. This means 'For the soul, all things are nothing to her. In her eyes, she herself is nothing. For her, only her God is everything.' (p. 655)

There is no doubt we would never start on a journey that meant giving up more for less. The word 'nothing' of itself would not lead anyone into action. If, however, we can have faith that the space created by the surrender of attachment will be filled with God, then the rewards are great indeed. So the answer is to put God first. John is not preaching a gospel of hatred for the creation, but he is saying that attachment to anything, whether good or bad, will keep us from reaching the summit.

We also need to realise what John means when he uses the term 'dark night'. John encourages us to view all the struggles and difficulties of life as coming from the hand of God, for the person's good.[4] Suffering can indeed be awful and in many cases comes through no fault of our own; however, 'all suffering can be seen as healing and in fact a great blessing; when you are burdened you are close to God, your strength, who abides with the

---

3. Iain Matthews, *The Impact of God* (London: Hodder and Stoughton, 1995), p. 40.
4. Iain Matthews, *The Impact of God* (London: Hodder and Stoughton, 1995), p. 78.

afflicted.' (p. 86) When speaking of the interior or exterior trials which God gives us, John says: 'We should accept them all as from God's hand as a good remedy and not flee from them.' (p. 669) We can learn that in our most difficult moments when we turn to God we are given renewed strength as we receive God's inflow of love and grace.

John explains that 'this dark night is an inflow of God's grace into the soul, which purges it of its habitual ignorance and imperfections, natural and spiritual, and which contemplatives call infused contemplation or mystical theology.'[5] For John, when it comes upon us, the night is a place which leaves us with no control and brings us into a place of not knowing. He associated the night as a place where we encounter mystery. This encounter is 'in the night not after the night'. No matter how it might feel to us, 'night' is seen by John as being the place of 'sheer grace' where God does his work of completely transforming the soul.

John's imprisonment and escape in Toledo is a demonstration in the physical world of what was happening to him in his spiritual world. All familiar things were stripped away. Yet he never lost faith. From his poems and writings it is clear that he was transformed spiritually during his imprisonment. When, after long struggle, he eventually made his escape he carried with him poems he had written during this time of transformation. The echo of this is in each line of the poem *The Dark Night*. John was able to acknowledge that the darkness was indeed 'sheer grace'. The poem sings of his faith, his love of God; his acknowledgement that in the night God was working to bring about his escape, escape from the world of the senses to union with God. The final line of the poem shows that his escape was complete on all levels as he writes: 'with all my cares among the lilies cast.'

John gives us a clear system of how the prayer life of the individual evolves. For John, all prayer is good and any method is good as long as it engages with Jesus. So he says we can use any prayer we want in any location we choose. 'One thing only is

---

5. Andrew Louth, *The Origins of the Christian Mystical Tradition* (Oxford: Oxford University Press, 1981), p. 179.

necessary: knowing how to deny yourself truly for Christ.'[6] In *The Ascent of Mount Carmel* John teaches that there is a time to allow prayer to simplify and become a 'loving attentiveness'. After many years of praying and meditating the time may come when the practices seem 'dry'. Something else is necessary but we do not know what. John teaches that 'dryness is now the outcome of fixing the senses on subjects that formerly provided satisfaction'. (p. 189) There comes a time when all forms of prayer and concepts must be left behind in favour of silence. As a relationship with another person deepens there is less and less need to speak or even to ask for things. Just being with them is enough.

Through John's words we can appreciate it is the same with our relationship with God. If the desire is to be still, then this is what is needed. Stillness is not idleness but a willingness to allow for a deeper communion with God. 'They must be content simply with a loving and peaceful attentiveness to God. All desires disquiet the soul and distract it from the peaceful, quiet, and sweet idleness of the contemplation that is being communicated to it.' (p. 382)

Through John's teaching we may come to recognise this level of prayer; a level where we do nothing but appreciate that the present moment is the presence of God. Realising, as John says, that 'Images cannot be an adequate, proximate means to God'. (p. 186) What is needed is attentive love, a desire just to be with Jesus, to be with him, loving him. John writes: 'They should just sit in the loving attention of God, without making specific acts. They should conduct themselves passively without efforts of their own but with a simple, loving awareness, as when opening one's eyes with loving attention.' (p. 686)

In this way we can be more ourselves in prayer, more in touch with what is really in our heart. All that is necessary is to be present and to realise the truth of John's words: 'Preserve a loving attentiveness to God with no desire to feel or understand any particular thing concerning him.' (p. 92) Night can indeed seem to be a dark place but with faith we can understand that there is

---

6. Iain Matthews, *The Impact of God* (London: Hodder and Stoughton, 1995), p. 99.

somewhere to go and that only God can take us there. In this way prayer can happen at any time or in any place once the mind and heart are turned to God.

The Living Flame of Love

John wrote *The Living Flame of Love* for Dona Ana de Penalosa, a lay women who was receiving spiritual direction from him. Having received the poem she asked him to write a commentary on the stanzas. The commentary which followed is, for many, John's finest mystical work. This is his poem to the Holy Spirit. John uses it to express his total love for and faith in God. He ardently wants to share this with others, to show how we are all called to union with God. He believed God helped him write the commentary as there were so many souls eager for this knowledge. In the poem John describes The Holy Spirit as a flame burning the soul; he likens the soul to a log of wood. As the flame ignites the wood; the wood in turn becomes flame. The commentary then states that the soul is now burning in the flame of love.

As he writes this commentary John is aware of how it will be received by some: 'I do not doubt that some people, not understanding this nor knowing the reality of it, will either disbelieve it, or think it exaggerated, or reckon it less than it in fact is.'[7] God's otherness is total, any description of him 'falls so far short of the goal that any 'like' has to be qualified with a greater 'unlike'.[8] Nothing can be said that would in any way define him.'

We have to accept that we cannot know God in the way we know other people or things. As scripture says, 'Something greater than the temple is here.' 'Christ is an unfathomable mine, with seam after seam of treasures.'[9] If God is so other then his friendship has to be given, it cannot be conquered. A Christian must wait until God gives them what they seek when he so desires.[10] This concept is not easy to accept; in fact, to accept it we must have total humility, the humility to simply wait. God is

---

7. Iain Matthews, *The Impact of God* (London: Hodder and Stoughton, 1995), p. 33.
8. ibid., p. 70.
9. ibid., p. 71.
10. ibid., p. 71.

totally transcendent, totally other. Yet there is something in our heart which cries out for God and like Augustine will not rest until it rests in him.

The Living Flame of Love

1. O living flame of love
that tenderly wounds my soul
in its deepest centre! Since
now you are not oppressive,
now consummate! If it be your will:
tear through the veil of this sweet encounter!

2. O sweet cautery,
O delightful wound!
O gentle hand! O delicate touch
that tastes of eternal life
and pays every debt!
In killing you changed death to life.

3. O lamps of fire!
in whose splendours
the deep caverns of feeling
once obscure and blind
now give forth, so rarely, so exquisitely,
both warmth and light to their Beloved.

4. How gently and lovingly
you wake in my heart,
where in secret you dwell alone;
and in your sweet breathing,
filled with good and glory,
how tenderly you swell my heart with love.

As a spiritual director John had the great gift of empathy. The pain that had moulded him had also endowed him with an extraordinary capacity to enter the heart of the other, and understand it. John was known as a 'listener'. He disapproved of those masters who spent all their time lecturing their novices, instead of recognising their level and guiding them accordingly. 'Those who guide souls should realise that the principal agent and guide and motive force in this matter is not them, but the Holy Spirit.'[11]

He listened because he wished to learn. His favourite way of teaching was to ask questions and draw the person further along the line of their answers. He said, 'God carries each person along a different road, so that you will scarcely find two people following the same route in even half of their journey to God.' Each person is 'a most beautiful and finely made image of God'.[12] 'If a person is seeking God, much more is her Beloved seeking her. The soul, then, should know that God is the principal agent in this matter. 'He acts as guide of the blind, leading the soul by the hand to the place it knows not how to reach (to supernatural things of which neither its intellect nor will nor memory can know the nature).' (p. 684) This journey is totally unique for each person, which means that we cannot know how another is being lead, all we have to do is follow faithfully the road God is leading us on, and trust that he will care for all others in the same way.

John further tells us that God is always gazing on the creation, and for God to gaze is to love. For the Christian this is the way to understand how God acts towards us. 'When the Father gazes, he gazes through his Son. The Son is his face, smiling upon the world.'[13] 'John's understanding is that God goes right into the deepest part of each of us and fills us with himself. God is always seeking us and 'intends to pursue his seeking to the very limit'.[14]

These words show how we have things the wrong way around: God is seeking us; we are the ones that are being sought. It is through God's grace that we have the desire to pray and the desire to know and love him. This makes it possible to begin to acknowledge that God's desire is to give good things to us. As John writes: 'The desire for God is the preparation for union with him.' (p. 683) All that is required of us is to believe, 'believe that God does want to give us himself, that he is giving us himself and that he means to pursue that gift through to its ultimate

11. ibid., p. 61.
12. ibid., p. 14.
13. ibid., p. 30.
14. ibid., p. 31.

consequences.'[15] Keeping our desires within realistic limits is not John's advice but rather, 'making God's generosity not my poverty the measure of my expectations.'[16]

'Passing beyond all that is naturally and spiritually intelligible or comprehensible, souls ought to desire with all their might to attain what in this life could never be known or enter the human heart.' (p. 161) It is indeed impossible for our mind to comprehend that God is seeking us. However, we can trust and resolve not to stop trusting, and make 'a lavish God, who does not hesitate, a horizon within which we choose to live our life'. (p. 34) Knowing that God is, indeed, seeking us means that turning to God in prayer and gratitude is the most natural thing in the world.

St John of the Cross died in December 1591. The world has changed since that time – as far as the physical world is concerned John would not recognise it were he to return today. The ideas and concepts which we take for granted and the knowledge gained over the last four hundred years are so completely different from what was accepted and known in the sixteenth century. So the question arises: how can reading the words of St John of the Cross be of any value to us in the twenty-first century? The answer may be that the spiritual world does not change and is not subject to the passing of time; so reading and reflecting on what John has to say is as relevant for us as we make our spiritual journey towards God as at any time during the last five hundred years.

Reading the words of St John of the Cross can be challenging and require patience and perseverance on our part. He is a spirit on fire with the love of God, and writes from intimate personal knowledge of the states he describes. For those of us who have not reached these spiritual heights, his message may sound incredible when we look at ourselves and the world around us using our finite heart and intellect. John tells of a God who has only one desire: the desire to give himself completely to each and every one of us.

---

15. ibid., p. 32.
16. ibid., p. 33.

Passages for reflection from the writings of St John of the Cross

Preparation for reflection:

- Choose a time when you are not likely to be disturbed.
- Sit in a comfortable position with the body relaxed.
- For a minute or two follow the exercise that John recommends: They should just sit in the loving attention of God, without making specific acts. They should conduct themselves passively without efforts of their own but with a simple, loving awareness, as when opening one's eyes with loving attention.

(p. 686)

Do not look for any results from this exercise or make any judgement on yourself. It provides an opportunity for the mind and heart to simply acknowledge the presence of God. Through this acknowledgement gratitude may arise; and gratitude is said to be the way to open the heart.

Read the words of the passage for reflection very slowly, this will give a better opportunity for the words to be heard. While reading the passages be aware of your inner responses. Ask yourself: do I agree with what is being said? If so take a moment to acknowledge this. If you do not understand, or disagree with something, also mark this.

𝒟 𝒟 𝒟

1st Passage for Reflection

John sums up his teaching in the following way:
In order to arrive at having pleasure in everything
desire to have pleasure in nothing
In order to arrive at possessing everything desire to possess nothing.
In order to arrive at being everything desire to be nothing.
In order to arrive at knowing everything desire to know nothing.[17]

---

17. Iain Matthews, *The Impact of God* (London: Hodder and Stoughton, 1995), p. 36.

Exercise:
What is your immediate response to the above lines?
Do you think that personal possessions are important?
Do you value your knowledge?
Could you live like this?

2nd Passage for Reflection

What more do you want, o soul! And what else do you search for outside, when within yourself you possess your riches, delights, satisfaction and kingdom – your beloved whom you desire and seek? Desire him there, adore him there. Do not go in pursuit of him outside yourself. You will only become distracted and you won't find him, or enjoy him more than by seeking him within you. (p. 480)

Exercise:
Where do you normally look for God?
When praying what usually distracts you?
What does it mean to seek Jesus within?

3rd Passage for Reflection

The following passage is long, so it will require time to read and reread in order to become familiar with it. This represents John at his most sublime, as he describes for us how through the grace of the Holy Spirit our souls becomes united with God.

The Living Flame of Love: Stanza 1

The soul's centre is God. When it has reached God with all the capacity of its being and the strength of its operation and inclination, it will have attained its final and deepest centre in God, it will know, love, and enjoy God with all its might. When it has not reached this point it still has movement and strength for advancing further and is not satisfied. Although it is in its centre, it is not yet in its deepest centre, for it can go deeper in God.

It is noteworthy, then, that love is the inclination, strength, and power for the soul in making its way to God, for love unites it with God. The more degrees of love it has, the more deeply it enters into God and centres itself in him. We can say that there are as many centres in God possible to the soul, each one deeper than the other, as there are degrees of love of God possible to it. A stronger love is a more punitive love, and we can understand in this manner the many mansions the Son of God declared were in his Father's house.

Hence, for the soul to be in its centre – which is God, as we have said – it is sufficient for it to possess one degree of love, for by one degree alone it is united with him through grace. Should it have two degrees, it becomes united and concentrated in God in another, deeper centre. Should it reach three, it centres itself in a third. But once it has attained the final degree, God's love has arrived in the soul in its ultimate and deepest centre, which is to illuminate and transform it in its whole being, power, and strength, and according to its capacity, until it appears to be God.

When light shines on a clean and pure crystal, we find that the more intense the degree of light, the more light the crystal has concentrated within it and the brighter it becomes; it can become so brilliant from the abundance of light received that it seems to be all light. And then the crystal is undistinguishable from the light, since it is illumined according to its full capacity, which is to appear to be light. (p. 645)

Exercise:
Having become familiar with the passage, start by marking words or sentences which stand out for you.
What meaning does this passage have in your life?
Do you accept that 'love is the inclination, strength, and power for the soul in making its way to God'?

4th Passage for Reflection

Apophatic theology, negative theology, is a theological system that attempts to describe the nature of God by focusing on what God is not rather than on what God is. It is believed that as God transcends human understanding the only way that we can get close to saying anything about the nature of God is to say what God is not.

St John of the Cross, whose writings are very much in the apophatic tradition, writes: '*The Dark Night* is the dark night of faith when images and concepts are stripped from the intellect as part of its preparation for union.'[18] This theme of 'unknowing' is found in many of his poems, for example his poem concerning the ecstasy experienced in high contemplation.

Poem concerning the ecstasy experienced in high contemplation

1. I entered into unknowing,
yet when I saw myself there,
without knowing where I was,
I understood great things;
I will not say what I felt
for I remained in unknowing
transcending all knowledge.

2. That perfect knowledge
was of peace and holiness
held at no remove
in profound solitude;
it was something so secret
that I was left stammering,
transcending all knowledge.

3. I was so overwhelmed,
so absorbed and withdrawn,
that my senses were left
deprived of all their sensing,
and my spirit was given
an understanding while not understanding,
transcending all knowledge.

4. He who truly arrives there
cuts free from himself;
all that he knew before
now seems worthless,
and his knowledge so soars

18. Andrew Louth, *The Origins of The Christian Mystical Tradition* (Oxford: Oxford University Press, 2007), p. 184.

that he is left in unknowing
transcending all knowledge.

5. The higher he ascends
the less he understands,
because the cloud is dark
which lit up the night;
whoever knows this
remains always in unknowing
transcending all knowledge.

6. This knowledge in unknowing
is so overwhelming
that wise men disputing
can never overthrow it,
for their knowledge does not reach
to the understanding of not
understanding,
transcending all knowledge.

7. And this supreme knowledge
is so exalted
that no power of man or learning
can grasp it;
he who masters himself
will, with knowledge in
unknowing,
always be transcending.

8. And if you should want to hear:
this highest knowledge lies
in the loftiest sense
of the essence of God;
this is a work of his mercy,
to leave one without
understanding,
transcending all knowledge.

(p. 53)

Exercise:

As the poem is so rich in meaning it will be necessary to take one verse at a time for reflection.

St John of the Cross says this poem is written to describe the ecstasy experienced in high contemplation.

First verse for reflection:

I entered into unknowing,
yet when I saw myself there,
without knowing where I was,
I understood great things;
I will not say what I felt
for I remained in unknowing
transcending all knowledge.

Exercise:

How can you understand great things and remain in unknowing?

Why would you not be able to say what you felt?

Continue with each verse in this way; asking questions which arise from the reflections.

5th Passage for Reflection

It is better to be burdened and in company with the strong than to be unburdened and with the weak. When you are burdened, you are joined to God. He is your strength, and he is with people who suffer. When there is no burden, you are just with yourself, your own weakness. It is in the difficulties which test our patience that the virtue and strength of the soul is increased and affirmed. (p. 85)

Exercise:

Is what John is saying in this passage within your own experience?

Can facing difficulties strengthen our spiritual life?

6th Passage for Reflection

Who can free themselves from lowly manners and limitations if you do not lift them to yourself, my God, in purity and love? How will human beings begotten and nurtured in lowliness rise up to you, Lord, if you do not raise them with the hand that made them?

You will not take from me, my God, what you once gave me in your only Son, Jesus Christ, in whom you gave me all I desire. Hence I rejoice that if I wait for you, you will not delay. (p. 87)

Exercise:
Is it possible to acknowledge that we can do nothing to raise ourselves to God?
Can you trust that God will give you all you desire?

7th Passage for Reflection

Have a great love for those who contradict and fail to love you, for in this way love is begotten in a heart that has no love. God so acts with us, for he loves us that we might love by means of the very love he bears towards us. Where there is no love, put love, and you will draw out love.

Exercise:
When you are in a situation where there is a lack of love might remembering these words help to change things?

Finally:

As you complete the study of the reflections on the writings and teachings of St John of the Cross, consider how they may help you on your personal spiritual journey.

❧ ❧ ❧

For Further Study:

The Collected Works of St John of the Cross, translated by Kieran Kavanaugh OCD and Otilio Rodriguez OCD (Washington: ICS Publications, 1991)

Meister Eckhart

Meister Eckhart
1260–1329

Few details of the personal life of Meister Eckhart are known to us. We have no idea what he looked like or what type of personality he had. Also, he has left us no descriptions of his own spiritual experiences. So unlike, for example, St Teresa of Avila who described in such detail the events of her spiritual journey, Eckhart does not speak of himself or of his own spiritual experiences. We come to know the man through his sermons. From these sermons it is possible to appreciate the depth of wisdom of this brilliant and original preacher. The Dominicans have always put great stress upon the role of preaching, and it was his preaching that people in large numbers came to hear. As preacher the focus was not on himself. Preaching was not about his experiences, mystical or otherwise. It was about his hearers, about their experiences and their lives. As he once put it:

> I say yet more (do not be afraid, for this joy is close to you and is in you); there is not one of you who is so coarse-grained, so feeble of understanding or so remote but they may find this joy with themselves, in truth, as it is, with joy and understanding, before you leave this church today, indeed before I have finished preaching: you can find this as truly within you, live it and possess it, as that God is God and I am a man.[1]

1. William Harmless SJ, *Mystics* (Oxford: Oxford University Press, 2008), p. 133.

Eckhart through his preaching was initiating his hearers into divine mystery, into the mystery that God dwells at the core of their identity as human beings. From words like these we get glimpses of the spiritual vision and love of wisdom of Eckhart.

Eckhart was born in Thuringia in Germany around the year 1260 and probably died 1329. It is believed that he was born into a family of the lower aristocracy. He entered the Dominican Priory at the monastery in Erfurt at the age of fifteen. As the Dominicans always placed great value on education this meant he received an excellent education with access to the finest libraries and the opportunity not only to study but also to teach and travel. After taking his vows he went to the University of Paris, where he studied Aristotle and the Platonists, and received a degree of Master of Arts. In 1294 he was elected Prior of his old convent at Erfurt and Vicar of Thuringia (the local representative of the Provincial). In 1303 he returned to Paris in order to take up the Dominican chair in theology. He twice held the chair in theology at the University of Paris, an achievement which he held in common with the greatest of Dominican theologians, St Thomas Aquinas.[2] In Paris he proved to be a very successful academic theologian and was also popular as an administrator.

He went to Strasburg in 1313 and was spiritual director there to the nuns of a ring of Dominican convents. It was here that his reputation as a preacher was built. He preached in the vernacular rather than in Latin, and has been called the 'father of modern German'. At this time it was usual for sermons to be preached in Latin which meant that the ordinary people did not understand what was being said. When it was argued that he should not teach such lofty things to the common people, Eckhart responded by claiming that the new vernacular theology was an important method of teaching, he said:

> And we shall be told that one ought not to talk about or write such teachings to the untaught. But to this I say that if we are not to teach people who have not been taught, no one will ever be

2. Oliver Davies, *Meister Eckhart: Selected Writings* (London: Penguin Books 1994), p. XII

taught, and no one will ever be able to teach or write. For that is why we teach the untaught, so that they may be changed from uninstructed into instructed.[3]

In 1325 the Dominicans in Venice heard with consternation rumours that one of their brethren in Germany was setting forth things in his sermons to the common people that might easily lead his listeners into error. This resulted in Eckhart being called before the Inquisition. In 1327 he appeared before the Franciscan Archbishop of Cologne to answer the charges brought against him. He was the first medieval theologian to be summoned on charges of heresy. He refuted the claims, insisting: 'If there is something false that I do not see in the passages or in my other remarks and writings, I am always ready to yield to a better understanding.' He further said that if erroneous statements were found in his writings or sermons, he would retract them, saying in his defence, 'I can be in error but I cannot be a heretic, because the first belongs to the intellect, and the second to the will.'[4] He was then, as always, loyal and obedient to the church, but the charges against him were not dropped. He appealed to Rome and started to walk the five hundred miles to Avignon (where the pope was living at the time), to plead his case at the papal court.[5] After his arrival in Avignon a commission was set up by the pope to examine some disputed passages of his writings. This went on for many months and during that time Eckhart, who would have been sixty-seven or sixty-eight at the time died in Avignon. There are no details of where he died or where he was buried.

Eckhart was never condemned as a heretic but after his death a papal bull was issued which spoke of papal fears of Eckhart's vernacular theology by expressly noting that his errors were 'put

---

3. Unless otherwise stated all quotations are taken from Bernard McGinn, *The Mystical Thought of Meister Eckhart* (New York: The Crossroad Publishing Co., 2001). All future references will indicate in brackets after each citation the page number. (p. 13)

4. William Harmless SJ, *Mystics* (Oxford: Oxford University Press, 2008), p. 113.

5. Ursula Fleming, ed., *Meister Eckhart: The Man from whom God hid nothing* (London: Fount Paperbacks, 1988), p. 15.

forth especially before the uneducated crowd in his sermons'. Towards the end of the bull the pope absolves Eckhart himself of heresy, noting that on the basis of a public document 'the aforesaid Eckhart professed the catholic faith at the end of his life and revoked and also deplored the twenty-six articles, which he admitted that he had preached ... insofar as they could generate in the minds of the faithful a heretical opinion, or one erroneous and hostile to the faith.'[6]

Since 1980 steps have been taken by the Dominican Order, supported by lay people and friends, to seek an official declaration from the pope in order to acknowledge the exemplary character of Eckhart's activity and preaching and to recommend his writings (particularly the spiritual works, treatises and sermons) as an expression of authentic Christian mysticism and as trustworthy guides to the Christian life according to the spirit of the gospel.

In 1985 members of this Commission were received in audience by Pope John Paul II. In his discourse with them the Holy Father told them he was very pleased with their work and went on to say: 'Did not Eckhart teach his disciples: "All that God asks you most pressingly is to go out of yourself – and let God be God in you"?' One could think that, in separating himself from creatures, the mystic leaves his brothers, humanity, behind. The same Eckhart affirms that, on the contrary, the mystic is marvellously present to them on the only level where he can truly reach them, that is in God.'[7] The fact that the Pope had acknowledged Eckhart in this way meant for practical purposes Eckhart's rehabilitation has been accomplished.

In the writings of Meister Eckhart we have examples of the apathetic or unknowing theology. As seen in the writings of St John of the Cross, writers of the apophatic tradition find their normal use of language insufficient to communicate their experiences, and so push themselves and their readers to the very edges

---

6. Reiner Schurmann, *Wandering Joy* (Great Barrington, MA: Lindisfarne Books, 2001), p. 229.

7. Ursula Fleming, ed., *Meister Eckhart: The Man from whom God hid nothing* (London : Fount Paperbacks, 1988), p. 19.

or boundaries of any existing systems in order to try to share those experiences with them. An example of this can be heard in the following words from one of Eckhart's sermons.

> God is something that must transcend being, date or location ... and although he is in all creatures, yet he is more than all of them. The divine One is a negation of negations and a desire of desires. What does 'One' mean? Something to which nothing is to be added. The soul lays hold of the Godhead where it is pure, where there is nothing beside it, nothing else to consider. The One is a negation of negations. Every creature contains a negation: one denies that it is the other ... But God contains the denial of denials. He is that One who denies of every other that it is anything except himself.[8]

In this passage Eckhart is demonstrating how our point of view differs from that of God's. For most of us, when we look at the creation we see others and think of them as different from ourselves. However, according to Eckhart's words the opposite is true for God. From the point of view of God, all is himself. Eckhart further states that:

> Once the birth of God in the soul has occurred, no creature can hinder you; instead they will all direct you to God and this birth ...Yes, all things become simply God to you, for in all things you notice and love only God, just as a man who stares long at the sun in heaven sees the sun in whatever he afterwards looks at.
>
> *(p. 64)*

Eckhart makes the point in his sermons that we do not have to gain anything in order to be united with God, all that is necessary is to 'chip' away at the things which cover this unity.

> When an artist makes a sculpture out of wood or stone, he does not put his idea into the wood but, rather he chips away the material that has been hiding it. He does not impart something to the wood but cuts the covering away and removes the tarnish so

8. Hastings Moore and Gary W. Moore, eds, *The Neighbourhood of Is* (Boston: University Press of America, 1984), p. 37.

that what was hidden there may shine. This is 'the treasure hid in a field'.[9]

One of the recurring themes in the Eckhart's sermons is the need to live in the present, in the now: Most of our troubles arise from thinking of what has happened in the past or becoming anxious about the future, and this causes us pain. However, the past and future do not in fact exist – all we have is the present moment. If we could live our life in this present moment, detached from the idea of past and future we would, he tells us, discover that this 'now' is always new.

> The now wherein God made the world is as near this time as the now I am speaking in this moment, and the last day is as near this now as was yesterday. The soul's day and God's day are different. In her natural day the soul knows all things above time and place; nothing is far or near. And that is why I say, this day all things are of equal rank. To talk about the world as being made by God tomorrow, yesterday, would be talking nonsense. God makes the world and all things in this present now.[10]

Living in the now is the way to experience true detachment according to Eckhart. True detachment he says means 'a mind so little moved by what befalls it, by joy and sorrow, honour and disgrace, as a broad mountain by a gentle breeze.'[11]

Eckhart places great emphasis on the need for rest; he stresses that to still the mind one must still the body too. He says 'the soul must rest in God', and illustrates this by saying 'stand over flowing water and you cannot see yourself. But supposing it is clear, then where it is collected and still enough for a reflection you can see your form in it. The first and noblest work of God is motionless, divine rest. It stands to reason that the maker of motionless is himself unmoved. Were God not unmovable there could nothing motionless be made.

---

9. ibid., p. 5.
10. F.C. Happold, *Mysticism* (Middlesex: Penguin Books Ltd, 1975), p. 279.
11. Ursula Fleming, ed., *Meister Eckhart: The Man from whom God hid nothing* (London: Fount Paperbacks, 1988), p. 15.

In all things I sought rest ... If I were asked to say to what end the creator has created creatures I should answer: Rest. And were I asked a second time. What are all creatures seeking so eagerly by nature? I should answer: Rest. And if a third time I were asked what the soul seeks in all her agitations, once more I should say: Rest.[12]

According to him, 'Nothing in all creation is so like God as stillness.'[13]

Eckhart lived in an age which placed great emphasis on penitential practices but this was not his way. Instead, for him, love was what was needed. He wrote 'penitential exercises were created because of the opposition between spirit and flesh in a fallen world. The body needs to be curbed by penance, but the bridle of love is a thousand times stronger. With love you overcome the body most surely, with love you load it down most heavily. Therefore God lies in wait for us with nothing so much as with love.' (p. 65) Through his writings we come to understand that for Eckhart there is complete certainty that nothing is closer to him than God. He says 'God is nearer to me than I am to my own self; my life depends on God's being near to me, present in me.'[14] This is what Eckhart hoped his audience would realise as they listened to his sermons. Realising this fundamental truth would, he believed, release them from fear and leave them free to enjoy the gift of life in all its abundance.

Meister Eckhart is a significant figure in the history of Christian mysticism. He has been referred to by several writers as 'The Man From Whom God Hid Nothing'. Almost seven hundred years have passed since he began preaching in his unique way. His words are as relevant today as they were then. Some of the statements in his sermons were guaranteed to shock his listeners; for instance when he said 'he prayed to God to rid him of God'. What he was referring to here of course, was the need to be rid of

---

12. ibid., p. 53.
13. Raymond Bernard Blakney, *Meister Eckhart* (New York: Harper & Row, 1957), p. 243.
14. Ursula Fleming, ed., *Meister Eckhart: The Man from whom God hid nothing* (London: Fount Paperbacks, 1988), p. 67.

the 'concept' of God, but his detractors were able to use statements like this and say they could generate in the minds of the faithful heretical opinion.

To read Eckhart is to be challenged both intellectually and spiritually. At first reading, his words can seem shocking, and it is clear that Eckhart did mean to shock people in order to wake them up. He wanted everyone to realise their true potential, which was, to experience the birth of God in their soul. The soul in which this birth takes place must be pure and peaceful; no longer bound to things of the world, living in the world but not of the world. 'Eckhart tells us that God 'must' give birth to himself in us fully at all times. He has no choice in the matter, this is simply his nature.'[15] This birth takes place in us when we become detached from the things of the world, when we let go, then the birth takes place. 'Detaching and birthing should be seen not as successive stages in a mystical path but as two sides of the same coin.' (p. 139)

When this happens, Eckhart assures us, we will be happy. People, he says, are happy when they are near God and the more they are aware of God the happier they are.

Since the middle of the nineteen century study of the works of Meister Eckhart has grown unabated and today seekers of truth, both Christian and non-Christian, alike are being drawn to his teachings. 'The growing host of new translations and studies over the past two decades indicates that the medieval Dominican, for all the controversy surrounding him and the difficulty of understanding his powerful message, continues to be a resource for all who seek deeper consciousness of God's presence.' (p. 2) A much read spiritual writer of our times, Eckhart Tolle, changed his name from Ulrich to Eckhart out of deference to the great man, and many of the points he makes in his popular book *The Power of Now* echo the teachings of Meister Eckhart.

---

15. Oliver Davies, *Meister Eckhart. Selected Writings* (London: Penguin Books 1994), p. XXIX.

Passages for reflection from the writings and sermons of Meister Eckhart

Preparation for reflection:

- Choose a quite time when you are not likely to be disturbed.
- Sit in a relaxed position with the body as free of tension as possible.
- Connect with listening … hear all the sounds.
- Be aware of the silence and stillness which underlies all the sounds.
- Accept everything as it is right now and just rest in the stillness.

1st passage for reflection

Humility exalts God and the more I have it, the more he is exalted and the more gently and sweetly his divine influence and gifts flow into me. That God is exalted by humility, I argue thus: The more I humble myself, the higher God rises above me. Humility is like a well. The deeper the well the higher he will stand who stands on the top. Similarly, the deeper I dig down into humility the more exalted God becomes and the more gently and sweetly his divine influence pours into me. That is why I must exalt God by humility.[16]

Exercise:

When Eckhart says 'humility is like a well' what is your understanding of this?

Remember the words 'humility exalts God' and see what effect this has on your attitude to yourself and others.

---

16. Raymond Bernard Blakney, *Meister Eckhart* (New York: Harper & Row, 1957), p. 234.

2nd Passage for Reflection

No person in this life may reach the point at which they can be excused from outward service. Even if they are given to a life of contemplation, still they cannot refrain from going out and taking an active part in life ... Thus, those who are given to the life of contemplation and avoid activities deceive themselves ... I say that the contemplative person should indeed avoid even the thought of deeds to be done during the period of their contemplation but afterwards they should get busy, for no one can or should engage in contemplation all the time, for active life is to be a respite from contemplation.

Since people cannot live without activities that are both human and various, we must learn to keep God in everything we do, and whatever the job or place, keep on with him, letting nothing stand in our way.

To be sure, this requires effort and love, a careful cultivation of the spiritual life, and a watchful oversight of all one's mental attitudes towards things and people. It is not to be learned by world-flight, running away from things, turning solitary and going apart from the world. Rather, one must learn an inner solitude, wherever or with whomsoever they may be. They must learn to penetrate things and find God there.[17]

> *Exercise:*
> In what way do you agree with Eckhart about the need for outward service?
> What does he mean by 'active life is to be a respite from contemplation'?
> Is it possible to learn to keep God in everything you do?
> What can you say about your experience of inner solitude?

3rd passage for reflection

God's endeavour is to give himself to us entirely. Just as fire seeks to draw the wood into itself and itself into the wood, it first finds

---

17. Hastings Moore and Gary W. Moore, eds, *The Neighbourhood of Is* (Boston: University Press of America, 1984), p. 73.

the wood unlike itself. It takes a little time. Fire begins by warming it, then heating it, and then it smokes and crackles because the two are so unlike each other. The hotter the wood becomes, the more still and quiet it grows. The more it is likened to the fire, the more peaceful it is, until it becomes entirely flame. That the wood be transformed into fire, all dissimilarity must be chased out of it. [18]

Exercise:
What is your initial understanding of what this passage is saying?
If the transformation of the wood into fire does take time, how can this analogy apply to your spiritual journey?
In what way does this passage describe your relationship with God?

4th passage for reflection

We should train ourselves to keep God always present in our mind, in our striving and in our love. Take note of how you are inwardly turned to God when in church or in your cell, and maintain the same attitude of mind, preserving it when you are among the crowd, into restlessness and diversity. And, as I often said, when we speak of sameness, we do not mean that we should regard all works as being the same, or all places and people. That would be wrong, for it is better to pray than to spin and a church is a worthier place than the street. But you should maintain the same attitude of mind in whatever you do, and the same trust and love for your God and the same seriousness of intent. Truly, if your attitude were always the same, then no one could prevent you from enjoying the presence of God.[19]

---

18. Reiner Schurmann, *Wandering Joy* (Great Barrington, MA: Lindisfarne Books, 2001), p. 90.
19. Oliver Davies, *Meister Eckhart: Selected Writings* (London: Penguin Books 1994), p. 9.

Exercise:
How can I train myself to keep God always present in my mind?
Do you have a different attitude depending on where you are and who you are with?
What prevents you from enjoying the presence of God?

5th passage for reflection

On no account let anyone suppose that they are far from God because of their faults or any other reason. If at any time your great shortcomings make an outcast of you and you cannot take yourself as being near God, take it then at any rate that he is near to you, for it is most mischievous to set God at a distance. Man goes far away or near but God never goes off; he is always standing close at hand, and even if he cannot stay within he goes no further than the door.[20]

Exercise:
What is this passage saying to you now?
Can you acknowledge God's nearness to you no matter what your state?

6th passage for reflection

One must here come to a transformed knowing, and this unknowing must not come from ignorance; rather, from knowing one must come into an unknowing. Then, we will become knowing with divine knowing and then our unknowing will be ennobled and clothed with supernatural knowing. And here, in that we are in a state of receiving, we are more perfect than if we were active.

For just as God is almighty in working, so too is the soul without ground in receiving, and therefore she is transformed with God and in God. God must act and the soul must receive. He

20. Ursula Fleming, ed., *Meister Eckhart: The Man from whom God hid nothing* (London: Fount Paperbacks, 1988), p. 32.

must know and love himself in her. She must know his knowledge and must love with his love, so that she is therefore more blessed with what is his than with what is hers; and also her blessedness is more dependent on his working than on her own. (p. 61–62)

Exercise:

Is it possible to understanding the need to move from knowing into unknowing, and how do you see this as a way forward on your spiritual journey?

Meister Eckhart says that God must act and the soul must receive. In what way can this instruction be made practical in your life now?

7th passage for reflection

Towards the end of his life Meister Eckhart's good friends bade him: 'Since you are going to leave us, give us one last word.' 'I will give you', he replied 'a rule which is the stronghold of all I have ever said, in which are lodged all the truths to be discussed or put into practice.'

It often happens that what seems trivial to us is more important to God than what we think important. Therefore, we ought to take everything God puts on us evenly, not comparing and wondering which is more important. We ought simply to follow where God leads, that is, to do what we are most inclined to do, to go where we are repeatedly admonished to go – to where we feel most drawn. If we do that, God gives his greatest in our least and never fails.

Now, some people despise the little things of life. It is their mistake, for they thus prevent themselves from getting God's greatness out of these little things. God is every way, evenly in all ways, to him who had eyes to see. But sometimes it is hard to know whether one's inclinations come from God or not, but that can be decided this way: If you find yourself always possessed of a knowledge or intimation of God's will, which you obey before everything else, because you feel urged to obey it and the urge is frequent, then you may know that it is from God. Some people want to recognise God only in pleasant enlightenment, and then they get pleasure and enlightenment but not God.

Some may ask: If God is in all ways and all things evenly, do I not still need a special way to get to him? Let us see. Whatever the way that leads you most frequently to awareness of God, follow that way; and if another way appears, different from the first, and you quit the first and take the second, and the second works, it is all right. To this end all kinds of activities may contribute and any work may help. However it would be better if one might take God and enjoy him in any manner and not have to hunt around for a special way: *This has been my joy.*[21]

> *Exercise:*
> Do you sometimes takes things as important which in hindsight are not?
> How are you grateful to God for all the 'small' things in your life?
> Is this passage helpful in describing how you can recognise the will of God in your life?
> Can you take God and enjoy him in any manner or at any time and not just on special occasions?

Finally:
Reflect on what you find most useful to your own spiritual journey in the writings of Meister Eckhart.

🌿 🌿 🌿

For further study:
There are a wide selection of books available on the writings of Meister Eckhart. A good book to start your study is *Meister Eckhart. Selected Writings*, translated by Oliver Davies, (London: Penguin Books, 1994).

---

21. Raymond Bernard Blakney, *Meister Eckhart* (New York: Harper & Row, 1957), p. 249.

Conclusion

꒰ ꒰ ꒰

The four mystics we have studied lived and worked in a very different world than the world we live in today. Many advances in technology and medicine have made life easier in the twenty-first century and most of us, in the developed world, can expect to live long and healthy lives. What is difficult to achieve today is time for silence and solitude, which was so important for the spiritual development of the mystics. Our days are filled with sounds and activities of one type or another, the television with its twenty-four-hour news, the internet, mobile phone, Facebook, the list goes on. We can do business and go shopping seven days a week, so that when Sunday comes there is little or no change in our activities. Living like this appears normal, and we can come to believe that it is necessary to be engaged in endless activities of one kind or another in order to live a full life. It is easy to see how the task of following in footsteps of the mystics can seem difficult, if not impossible.

The question is how is it possible to be a mystic and at the same time continue to participate in the modern world? Karl Rahner's view on this is reassuring. He writes: 'Every Christian is called to a mysticism of everyday faith, hope and love that differs only in degree, and not in kind, from the extraordinary experiences of recognised mystics. Mysticism is thus not limited to those who are technically called mystics in the Christian tradition.'[1] As most of us have no desire to become hermits or to abandon our everyday life, it is reassuring to read these words.

From reading the stories of the lives of the mystics and coming to appreciate what they say, we may find ourselves connecting with something that lies hidden, deep within our hearts. We may understand and appreciate what they are saying as if we already knew it, but accept that we could never articulate it for ourselves. This is the value of their writings; to lead us to discover truths, already known within us. Meister Eckhart tells us not to worry about what we do but rather what we are:

> People should not worry so much about what they do but rather about what they are. If they and their ways are good, then their deeds are radiant. If you are righteous, then what you do will also be righteous. We should not think that holiness is based on what we do but rather on what we are, for it is not our works which sanctify us but we who sanctify our works.[2]

Realising this can help us to begin to make sacred every moment of our life and to understand that we can connect with God at any time and in all our activities and not just when we are praying or in church.

All through our life we have needs. We pray for help with these needs to find solutions and answers. However, St John of the Cross tells us these needs are just symptoms of a greater need which is our need for God. We ache because of this and nothing will satisfy us or fill this space for us but God. This need for God and the knowledge that nothing but God will satisfy us gives us the sense of always being incomplete. This has always been the case for human beings when they begin to appreciate their need for God. As St Augustine wrote: 'Our hearts are restless until they rest in you.'

---

1. Declan Marmion, *A Spirituality of Everyday Faith* (Louvain: Peeters Press, 2007), p. 62
2. Oliver Davies, *Meister Eckhart: Selected Writings* (London: Penguin Books 1994), p. XII

In our world we can be aware of many injustices, and many good causes which call for our attention. There are also people who respond to the needs of others with their money, their time and even with their life. All who work in this way are wonderful examples of how the human spirit naturally desires to do good and to serve others. Without undermining these works it is helpful to be reminded by St John of the Cross of 'the one thing the Bridegroom said is necessary', that is attentiveness to God. Without this there is always the risk of doing the work of the Lord but forgetting the Lord of the work. St John of the Cross points out the need for another way: a way of living which has love of God at its very centre. He writes: 'For a little of this pure love is more precious to God and the soul and more beneficial to the church, even though it seems one is doing nothing, than all these other works put together.' (p. 587) He speaks of the need to spend time each day praying and meditating. This may appear to be a solitary occupation which will be of benefit to no one but yourself. However, the effect of these times of silence and stillness on the greater community is immeasurable.

Mystics all teach of the value of sufferings in our life. Meister Eckhart says that God must be true to his word and he has told us in St John's gospel that our sorrow shall be turned into joy. In his *Book of Divine Consolation* Eckhart writes:

> Now, truly, if I knew for certain that all the stones in my possession were going to turn into gold, then the more stones I had and the bigger they were, the happier I would be. Indeed, I would ask for more stones and, if I could, would get big ones and many of them. In this way we would certainly be consoled in our grief.[3]

It would be unnatural for us to deliberately seek out suffering, and this is not what we should take from passages such as this, but when we do meet trials it is our attitude to them which is all important. For each Christian, the cross and the resurrection are a necessary part of their journey to God. Each of the mystics we have studied experienced suffering both physically and mentally.

---

3. ibid., p. 68.

However, it was the way they met this suffering that transformed their lives.

It is worth noting that as mystics such as Julian of Norwich lived their life of prayer and service to their communities they were unaware how people many hundreds of years later would still be benefiting from their examples. As spiritual teachers, she and others like her continue to provide us with a spiritual road map, they point the way forward and also point out possible pit falls on the way. With their guidance and their experience of how our prayer life develops, they provide us with help and assistance which is invaluable. All the mystics speak to us of God, and the common thread running between them is the declaration that God is love, and that the experience of God is freely available to us through grace. This grace, offered freely to us, can of course be accepted or rejected.

St John of the Cross writes: 'Our point of greatest openness on to God is our desire: What prepares the person to be united with God is the desire for God.'[4] This desire is not thinking about God, but a way of living which has devotion to God as its very centre. He also wrote of how when this is realised our whole life and way of seeing things is turned around: 'And here lies the remarkable delight of this awakening. The soul knows creatures through God and not God through creatures. This amounts to knowing the effects through their cause and not the cause through its effects.' (p. 710) Hearing these words it is clear that he himself realised this state of being, and was writing so that others might realise it too.

To come to know what we are, we have to come out of what we are not; for this to happen we need to take time each day to visit our own interior castle. For each, the important thing is to find a way of doing this which is best suited to us. We can enter into our interior world by reading scripture, reflecting, praying, meditating and by periods of silence. In this way we are providing nourishment for our minds and hearts and establishing a way of living which has God at its centre.

---

4. Iain Matthews, *The Impact of God* (London: Hodder and Stoughton, 1995), p. 150.

Each day we can choose whatever prayers, method of meditating, passages of scripture, or words of a mystic which we find helpful and which we most connect with. As Meister Eckhart says: 'Whatever the way that leads you most frequently to awareness of God, follow that way.' We can start with a few minutes each day; the important thing is not the length of time spent but the regular practice. Remember to practice the exercise of falling still before starting. Also, when reading, continue to read the words slowly to allow them to touch you personally, to speak directly to you. By taking time out like this, we come to understand that stillness is necessary in order to connect with the centre of our inner world, the heart, which is the seat of our emotions. This is where love resides. As scripture says: 'Be still and know that I am God.' No matter how much work one does on the level of the mind, the truth is we can never know God through the mind, love alone is what is needed.

Julian of Norwich wrote: 'Before God made us he loved us, which love has never abated and never will. And in this love he has done all his works, and in this love he had made all things profitable for us, and in this love our life is everlasting.' (p. 342, LT) As we move into deeper stillness and silence, the hope is that the full meaning of these words will become evident to us.

The rich heritage of our Christian mystical tradition, which includes the mystics we have studied, offers us the possibility of participating here and now in the real and eternal life. Through their teachings, the mystics bring us closer to the certainty of God's presence in our life. As we come to appreciate this presence we are set on the same road they followed and can, through our efforts, however little or imperfect they are at first, journey to God and experience a life lived in the fullest, deepest sense that is possible for us.

Selected bibliography

Agnew, Una and Flanagan, Bernadette, eds, *Transformative Reading in With Wisdom Seeking God: Studies in spirituality series* (Leuven: Peeters, 2008)

Father John-Julian OJN, *A Lesson of Love (The Revelations of Julian of Norwich)* (London: Darton, Longman & Todd, 1988)

Fleming, Ursula, *Meister Eckhart: The Man from whom God hid nothing* (London: Fount Paperbacks, 1988)

Happold, F.C., *Mysticism* (Middlesex: Penguin Books Ltd, 1975)

Harmless SJ, William, *Mystics* (Oxford: Oxford University Press, 2008)

Louth, Andrew, *The Origins of the Christian Mystical Tradition* (Oxford: Oxford University Press, 1981)

Matthews, Iain, *The Impact of God* (London: Hodder and Stoughton, 1995)

McGinn, Bernard, *The Mystical Thought of Meister Eckhart* (New York: The Crossroad Publishing Co., 2001)

Nuth, Joan M., *Wisdom's Daughter* (New York: The Crossroad Publishing Co., 1991)

Schurmann, Reiner, *Wandering Joy* (Great Barrington, MA: Lindisfarne Books, 2001)

Works of the Mystics:

Julian of Norwich (Showings), trans. Edmund Colledge OSA and James Walsh SJ (New Jersey: Paulist Press, 1997)

The Collected Works of St Teresa of Avila, vol. I, trans. Kieran Kavanaugh OCD and Otilio Rodriguez OCD (Washington: ICS Publications, 1987)

The Collected Works of St John of the Cross, trans. Kieran Kavanaugh OCD and Otilio Rodriguez OCD (Washington: ICS Publications, 1991)

Meister Eckhart: Selected Writings, trans. Oliver Davies (London: Penguin Books, 1994)